To Mary Joy

DRISHANE CONVENT

This book is dedicated to

The Infant Jesus Sisters Ireland 1909-2009

First published in 2009 by
IJS Centenary Committee
www.ijs.ie

ISBN
978-0-9562456-0-1

Design and Production by
Origin Design, Dublin.
www.origin.ie

Printed in Ireland by
W&G Baird

Infant Jesus Sisters
Ireland 1909-2009

The Voyage Out

Catherine KilBride & Deirdre Raftery

4

CONTENTS

INTRODUCTION

This book has been written to mark the centenary in 2009 of the arrival of the Infant Jesus Sisters in Ireland. It is our hope that the book not only contributes to the spirit of celebration, but also to documenting some of the history of the Institute. It is a story that is rich with resonances of the social, political and religious changes of the twentieth century, and that reflects the 'voyage out' of the Irish Sisters, as they worked in Asia, Africa, Australia, Europe and the Americas.

The idea for a book developed in February 2008, when Sr Rosemary Barter, Provincial Superior, gathered a group of Sisters and past pupils together in Mallow to discuss ideas for the centenary celebrations ahead. We tentatively suggested that some form of publication might be worth thinking about, although everyone could see that neither a history of the Institute nor a full-scale study of its foundations in Ireland could be accomplished in such a short time. A shorter volume might, we suggested, be prepared in time for May 2009. As a first step we volunteered to examine the Infant Jesus Archives in Dublin and see what records and images were stored there. We found letters, Annals and planning documents which helped us to understand why the Sisters came to Ireland in the first place, and how they set about founding Drishane. Written in French, in beautiful script, and carefully preserved, these papers yielded up some sense of the extraordinary vision and energy that characterised those who were at the very centre of the planning for Drishane in the early twentieth century.

After our preliminary survey of the Dublin Archives, it became clear to us that the whole spirit of mission, dating back to the nineteenth century, was probably only to be found in important documents located at the Archives Nicolas Barré in Paris. In June 2008, we went to the Mother House in Paris and did an intensive survey of all the papers relating to the founding of Drishane. The Archives also held photographs and written accounts that captured some of the experience of the early generations of Drishane Sisters who went out to the missions, as well as Irish Sisters who had gone out long before the founding of Drishane.

Having carefully considered the range of material in Dublin and Paris, we decided that we would attempt a publication that would give readers a taste of the riches that we had seen. The aim was to let some of these documents and images 'speak' for themselves, while we would also provide a documentary account of developments and changes within the Irish foundations. The book, we concluded, would not be an interpretive study of the Institute in Ireland, nor would it be an historical evaluation of the work of women religious. These types of studies, which demand extensive research over a sustained period of time, are perhaps less suited to the spirit of the centenary celebration that Sr Rosemary had envisaged.

The book comprises three parts. Part One examines the building stages of the foundations in Ireland: Drishane, Malahide and Ballyferriter. Part Two charts the start of the 'voyage out' to the missions, undertaken by successive groups of Drishane Sisters. Part Three looks at the ways in which the Sisters accommodated change and developed initiatives, after the Second Vatican Council.

Readers will encounter several different referents for the Sisters: in the seventeenth century they were the 'Charitable Mistresses of the Holy Infant Jesus, known as the Dames de St Maur'; this was shortened frequently to the 'Dames de St Maur' which therefore appears in many documents and publications; 'Sisters of the Holy Infant Jesus' and 'Infant Jesus Sisters' were introduced later. The recent and more informal term, 'IJ Sisters' or 'IJS', is sometimes found in contemporary documents, and in conversations with the Sisters and their friends. In this book, we use the terms exactly as they were encountered in the documented or oral contexts. Some Sisters were titled 'Sr St' upon the Reception of the Habit, and the use of 'St' continued until 1962 after which time it was dropped completely. Sisters were given a 'name in religion' at Reception but, with the changes that followed the Second Vatican Council, many Sisters chose to return to using their Christian names. For clarity in this book, when a Sister is mentioned for the first time we give her title and name in religion, followed by her Christian name, surname and address in parenthesis. At the point in the book where Sisters have discontinued the use of 'St', we discontinue its use. At the point where a Sister has changed her name back to her Christian name, we follow suit. Our attempt to use terms that are historically accurate extends to references to places. So, for instance, in the early part of the book we adopt the Sisters' references to 'Malaya' but we commence the use of 'Malaysia' for material after 1963.

Once we had decided upon the scope of the book, there began the task of completing it in time for May 2009. This task was eased by the support of people to whom we owe a debt of gratitude. Sr Elisabeth Sondag, archivist in Paris, was most generous with her time and her great knowledge of the collection which is in her expert care. Sr Colette Flourez and the Communauté Nicolas Barré made us so welcome during our stay at the Mother House in Paris. Brigitte Appavou at the Archives Missions Etrangères de Paris was most helpful with biographical information and photographs of Père Charles Nain. In Dublin, archivist Marie French and Sr Pauline O'Dwyer were constant sources of information. In the summer of 2008, we interviewed several Sisters in Cork; our thanks to these Sisters and to Sr Mairéad O'Sullivan, Sr Beatrice Ahern and Sr Florence O'Sullivan who welcomed us to their Communities; our thanks also to Sr Marie Pitcher, Superior General of the Institute, who gave generously of her time, and to all the Sisters who agreed to be interviewed. We are deeply grateful to Melissa KilBride for her help with the preparation of the final manuscript; to Garrett Bennis of Origin for his vision, his enthusiasm and his commitment to the project; and to Michelle Cooper-Galvin who generously supplied all the modern photography for Part Three. The funding for the production of this book by IRD Duhallow LEADER Programme is gratefully acknowledged.

Finally, we thank Sr Rosemary Barter, Provincial Superior, for her faith in our work and her support throughout the past year. While she gave us open access to the Archives, Sr Rosemary exercised no editorial control, so any errors and omissions in this book are our own.

Catherine KilBride and Deirdre Raftery
May 2009

FOREWORD

When the first Sisters arrived in Drishane in March 1909, their ambition was to establish a foundation in Ireland which would provide English-speaking Sisters for the missionary work of the congregation in Malaysia, Singapore and Japan. They were more than successful in this aim, and were eventually to send Sisters to Australia, Thailand, the Americas, and Africa.

The first part of this book charts the establishment of two schools in Ireland, at Drishane and Malahide, as well as the foundation in Ballyferriter, Co. Kerry, while the second part documents the voyage of the Sisters to their overseas mission. When the Sisters arrived in Ireland in 1909, they could not have envisaged the changes that were to take place in the Church during the second half of the century. The third part of the book captures some of the creative ways with which the Sisters embraced change, and responded to it with a renewed zeal, while seeking to remain true to the founding spirit of the Institute.

Catherine KilBride and Deirdre Raftery, past pupils respectively of our schools in Drishane and Malahide, have kindly offered to produce this very beautiful commemorative book, which will surely help to keep the story alive. We are deeply grateful to both of them for the generosity with which they undertook all the necessary research for this painstaking work. They have captured very well the spirit of faith and courage, evident in the lives of so many women, who through the years have courageously and generously given their lives for others.

My hope is that this story may also speak to all who read it and lead to a renewed impetus in our way of living the Gospel message today.

Rosemary Barter IJS
Province Leader

Drishane Castle

Le domaine de Drishane
superficie de 250 acres, c-a-d.
toy peut décomposer ainsi :

A. Prés Terrains d'agri
environ 200 acres, c

B. Forêt bois - sapins, c
environ 25acres, c-a

C. Château dépendances
loges écoles routes e
environ 25 acres, c-a

Ressources principales à

PART ONE

Building

CONTENTS

Douglas Hall.

Vendredi 2 oct
1908.

Très Honorée Mère,

Arrivée hier mat.
à Douglas Hall, je
suis à voir aussi
que possible le dom.
de Drisham Cast.
et nous partions M...
que trois jour M...
les dans l'après...

Père Charles Bénédict Nain
Missions Étrangères de Paris 1870-1916

4º Saw-mill

Les mêmes opinants que
sur les trolleys.

Les questions à examiner sont
Marcheront elles à l'eau ou à
l'électricité ? (même remarque que
plus haut au sujet de l'énergie électrique)
L'ancienne bâtisse peut-elle
servir ? — Si non, où et comment
se ferait la nouvelle installation ? — Où se procurera-t-on les
scies ? — Organisation du personnel
— Débouché pr la fabrication.

Conseils à la chère petite Rde Mère

Préparez bien chaque conférence
avec Mr & Mme Anthony

Faites par écrit un questionnaire
bien net de tout ce que vs voulez
savoir — Ne vs gênez pas pr faire
vos objections et dire que vs ne comprenez
Prenez note des réponses — exigez du
net du positif — des preuves surtout
avant de donner ou la commande
les scies par exemple, ou le travail
de l'installation, demandez les prix

Mother St Claire Bringeon
Drishane's first Reverend Mother 1909-1926

THE FOUNDATION OF DRISHANE

PLANNING

> The Bishop's view, as you know, all along has been, and is, that he is granting a
> great favour in allowing the Nuns, who are not required to supply any diocesan
> want, to establish a foundation in his diocese.[1]

It was 1909 and the plan to establish themselves in Ireland was not going well for the
Infant Jesus Sisters. They had a presence in Malaya for fifty years. They were opening
schools at a remarkable rate and they could see the enormous potential for growth in their
missionary effort there, in Singapore (which was at that time still a part of Malaya) and in
Japan. The single obstacle to that growth was lack of personnel. They needed a substantial
and steady supply of qualified English-speaking teaching sisters. Having been founded in
France in 1662, they had survived the French Revolution and now had another battle on
their hands in France in the form of secularization. They had hoped that their English
houses in Wolverhampton and Weybridge would prove fruitful and, indeed, there were
some vocations, but not the numbers they had envisaged. Ireland just had to work out for
them. It would take more than an unwelcoming bishop to deter them. They had a pretty
formidable team and they were in no doubt at all that God was on their side.

PÈRE CHARLES NAIN,
MISSIONS ETRANGÈRES DE PARIS

A key member of their team was Père Charles Nain, a talented and sophisticated strategist.
The Séminaire des Missions Etrangères is in rue du Bac, just around the corner from the
Mother House of the IJ Sisters at 8 rue Abbé Grégoire in Paris. He had spent many years
in Singapore and, while serving in the Church of SS Peter and Paul there, was the architect
for the IJ convent chapel (completed in 1904) among other significant religious houses.

The first document in his hand-writing, although undated and incomplete, sets out
clearly the need to establish a novitiate in Ireland.[2] He states that religious vocations are
numerous, particularly in Kilkenny and Cork. Indeed, according to Père Nain, there was
hardly a family in Ireland who had not got a member in a religious order. He was sure
that there were Irish candidates who would be well suited to the missions in the Far East.
However, he advised that since particular circumstances prevailed in Ireland, the Sisters
would have to adapt their rules and discipline to the customs of the country.[3] There were
convents in existence in Ireland on which the IJ Sisters should model themselves. So,
they should establish a presence in Ireland and two or three Irish religious, who had the
required qualities and who already had experience of the Missions, should be members
(at least for a while) of the founding group. He stressed that it was these Irish sisters who

---

[1] IJAD, Canon Casey to Mr Duggan, 18th January 1909.
[2] IJAD, Père Nain Papers, 1908-1909.
[3] Perhaps the first example of this adaptation to local conditions is recorded in the account of Mother General St Henri's first official
visit in 1909 when, 'recognizing the demands made by the climate on issues such as sleep, and realizing that French Orders
established in Ireland had put back by an hour their rising time' the decision was taken to put back the rising time in Drishane also.

would attract candidates; they would produce a favourable impression on their compatriots and also on the ecclesiastical authorities.

These latter were trying to stop emigration from Ireland, according to Père Nain. They were equally opposed, in principle, to the departure of religious to foreign missions. He claimed that they had very good reason for this. American religious orders had been recruiting widely in Ireland for a number of years, with the result that hundreds if not thousands of young women who felt that they might have a religious vocation had left for the United States of America. Many of them discovered when they got there that the religious life was not for them. Unfortunately, he claimed, they were not supported by the religious orders when they made the decision to leave and were left high and dry, far from home. The consequence of this experience was that the Irish bishops were not well disposed to foreign religious and did not approve of their recruitment methods.

CONSIDERATION OF VARIOUS POTENTIAL PROPERTIES

Rochestown, County Cork

Père Nain had seen at first hand the work of the IJ Sisters in Singapore and had been particularly impressed by Sr St Beatrice (Margaret Foley, Cork) whom he met there. Her brother-in-law, Mr Cornelius Duggan who lived in Cork, was given the task of identifying possible properties in Ireland. From then he was the principal negotiator and agent for the Sisters in Ireland. He was fully committed to the task of finding them the most suitable property, on the best possible terms. The first potential property was in Rochestown, three miles from Cork city. Old Court, described as a castle, was in bad condition, not having been lived in for seven or eight years. Père Nain came to Ireland and visited the property in Rochestown. He described it as coming with 200 hectares of meadows and woodland. In a letter to Mother St Henri Deruelle, who was Mother General throughout the purchase period, he mentioned the main advantage as being that Old Court was 'near a Franciscan monastery', which meant that the Sisters could be assured of daily Mass. This proximity to another religious house, and in particular the opportunity that would provide of sharing a chaplain, was a serious consideration. It is particularly interesting in view of the enormous difficulties involved later in the provision of a chaplain for Drishane. Indeed, the salary of the chaplain was to become a stumbling block in the acceptance of the IJ Sisters in the Diocese of Kerry. In any event, he added that Old Court was really dilapidated and quite a lot of money would have to be spent on restoring the building.

Père Nain returned to Paris from Ireland, convinced that a foundation would succeed very well there and would bring many candidates for the religious life. He was surprised to find in Ireland no convent forming missionaries to work among the pagan peoples. While noting that numerous candidates for the religious life left every year for the United States, he found no convent dedicated to what he considered the real apostolate, the mission to 'idolators'.

In a letter to Mother General dated 30th June 1908[4], he remarked that the Irish people were generous and devoted to their faith, so he advised Mother St Henri to play to these two virtues in the clergy. She should, he suggested, present a proposed Irish novitiate as a partial substitute for the one that was closed in Paris by the secularizing French government. This would have a better chance of attracting the sympathy of the clergy: they always welcome with open arms the persecuted, 'especially ladies', he wrote. Secondly, Mother General should let them know that she would be investing the Congregation's funds in Ireland in order to save them from the greedy government in France. That too would appeal to the Irish, in his view.

On the other hand, because the Irish clergy were opposed with all their might to emigration, even if it was of religious sisters, he advised that it would be best not to mention the requirement to find postulants for the Far East; the sisters should keep these prayers in their hearts without committing them to paper.

Chaffpool House, County Roscommon

Another possible property identified by Mr Duggan was Chaffpool House near Ballaghadereen in County Roscommon. Several visits were paid there, starting before the foundation of Drishane and continuing even after that, by Père Nain as well as by Mother St Marguerite Marie (Assistant Mother General) and Sr St Anthony (Hannah Coleman, Tiernanean, Bandon, Co. Cork).[5] The house came with a few hundred acres. However, Mr Duggan felt that the price being asked was too high for what was on offer. Apart from about thirty acres of pasture land, the rest was uncultivated bogland and seventy acres of woodland. Père Nain counselled caution, expressing particular concern about the remote location. Ballymote, the nearest town, was six miles away. He pointed out, in an undated letter to Mother St Marguerite Marie, probably written at the time of their arrival in Drishane, that even getting daily provisions would prove difficult. The remarkable thing about the correspondence is that it continued for about six months after their founding of Drishane. Even when faced with all the challenges of establishing themselves in a new location, in a new country, they were still considering opening a second convent simultaneously. Canon Casey, parish priest of Millstreet, was strong in his condemnation of that as a strategy:

> I have only to repeat what I said more than once – that scattering forces in a new country is hardly ever prudent or successful. I think they ought to concentrate their energies in Drishane where they have a sufficiently wide field for their zeal and strength. If they attempt too much in the beginning they may end by not satisfying themselves or pleasing anyone.[6]

The plan to establish a second foundation in Ireland was abandoned for the time being. It emerged again in the 1940s and concluded in the establishment of Malahide in 1958.

---

[4] IJAD, Père Nain to Mother General St Henri, 30th June 1908.
[5] IJAP, 6M 2-1 Drishane 1909-1967, Fr Daly on behalf of the Bishop of Achonry, Dr Lyster, to Mother St Marguerite Marie, 12th July 1909.
[6] IJAD, Canon Casey to Mr Duggan, 23rd February 1909.

PLANS FOR THE ESTABLISHMENT
OF A CONVENT IN DRISHANE

Père Nain finally got to see Drishane on the 1st October 1908. He arrived in Cork from Paris in the morning, left straight away for Drishane in the afternoon, and wrote to Mother General the following morning expressing his amazement at everything he had seen.[7] Nature and human effort had worked together to make of that corner of Ireland a real heaven on earth. It would be hard to find a place more contemplative, more poetic too and also more suited to the silence and calm of religious life, he wrote. He loved the medieval tower, the castle, the setting. But, being the intelligent man he was, he immediately saw the potential of the estate and was convinced that it would be foolish to hesitate for a moment: it was essential to acquire this beautiful property. In his inimitable fashion, he drew up a document which is both a detailed inventory of the property, listing the actual as well as the potential income from it, and a plan for its development, with advice for Mother General as to how she should proceed in order to get the most from the property.

[7] IJAD, Père Nain to Mother General St Henri, 2nd October 1908.

c. Château dé[...]
loges écu[...]
&nviron [...]

Ressources princip[...]
1º Terrains. —

Nº Ter[...]

Les prés du domain[...]
à differents. Tenants.
&n Irlande la location
cation pour l'année en
bail tacite s'il [...]
en cas de difficultés.

(a). soit W meadow in[...]
(b). soit W grazing
(c) soit les deux à [...]
La vente des fo[...]
le droit de pâtura[...]
On conseille de n[...]

dances, lacs, fours à chaux

outes etc...

res, c.-à-d. 11 hectares.

—————

à retirer du domaine.

Bois. — 3° Industries diverses.

—— . ——

ns et prairies.

—————

et ces plusieurs lots et peuvent se louer

te fait que pour 11 mois, car la lo

(12 mois) séjour viendrait à une espèce de

difficile d'expulser le locataire

rd ou on loue =

c.-à-d. la récolte des foins

-d. le droit de pâturage

ois.

apporte entre £2 et £3 par acre.

apporte environ £2 par acre.

faire la récolte des foins tous les ac

DRISHANE CASTLE [8]

The estate of Drishane Castle covers a surface area of 250 acres, that is to say, almost 102 hectares which can be split up as follows:

A. Meadows and agricultural lands about 200 acres i.e. 80 hectares
B. Forest, woods - fir, oak, ash, beech - about 25 acres i.e. 11 hectares
C. Castle, outbuildings, lakes, lime kilns, lodges, yards, roads etc.
   about 25 acres i.e. 11 hectares

Principal resources of the estate from which income can be generated:
   1 Lands   2 Woods   3 Various industries

I Lands and Meadows

The meadows on the estate are in several lots and can be let to different tenants. In Ireland rent is charged for just 11 months because rent for the entire year (12 months) would be considered equivalent to a lease and it would be difficult to evict the lessee if there were problems.

One sells or leases

(a) either the meadowing i.e. the saving of the hay
(b) or the grazing i.e. the right to the pasture
(c) or both of these together.

The sale of the hay brings in between £2 and £3 per acre. Grazing rights bring in about £2 per acre. The advice is not to make the hay every year so as not to impoverish the land: just a section of it would be cut every year. The regular income would consist of the sale of the hay (from a certain acreage) and the grazing rights for the whole of the 200 acres. At a minimum, the meadows would bring in annually £500 i.e. 12.500 frs.

II Woods and forests

The principal varieties of trees found on the estate are fir, oak, ash and beech. There are about 25 acres of woodland not counting the ornamental trees which will not be exploited. A mechanical sawmill driven by hydraulic power is sufficient to deal with most of the timber. A well-thought out plan, that is, using your judgment to cut a small amount each year, will result in minimal reduction in the value of these woods and will produce annual revenue of £200 or 5000 frs.

Comment The sawmill, costing nothing in motor energy, could be set up on a larger scale, so as to saw not only the timber from the estate but also from outside; that would provide a source of quite considerable profit.

---

[8] IJAD, Père Nain Papers, 1908-1909.

III Various industries already on the estate

1   **Creamery** A creamery let by the year brings in, in rent, £25 i.e. 625 frs.
    The rent is paid from the 29th September, and ends with 6 months notice.

2   **Lime kilns** Lime is something which is a prime necessity for agriculture throughout
    the south of Ireland. You can't have a harvest without lime in this country as you
    couldn't in France without manure. Soil lacking in lime must be given it artificially or
    else it will be sterile. Consequently, the English government, which is at the moment
    ending its regime of oppression and restoring ownership of their lands to the Irish
    people, is doing its best to resolve the problem. Experts are being sent all over the
    country to study the question and to have lime kilns built.

    Three splendid lime kilns exist on the Drishane estate, and an inexhaustible supply of
    limestone lies a short distance from the kilns. Some metres of rail line with 3 or 4
    wagons would allow the stone to be transported to the kilns at no cost. The
    government would have liked to buy these lime kilns but they could not be sold
    separately nor split off from the estate. Even though they have been idle for several
    years, these 3 lime kilns are in quite a good state of conservation and it would take
    very little to put them back in working order. In a few years the lime kilns will
    provide the most important revenue on the whole estate.

    Here are some details on the lime kilns. They are of different sizes supplying:

    > The biggest, 80 barrels of lime a day;
    > The middle one, 60;
    > The smallest, 40.

    The daily output from the three kilns would be 180 barrels.

    Counting 300 working days, the kilns would produce 54,000 barrels annually.
    The barrel sells at 1/6 giving, after the deduction of costs, a profit of 6 pence or
    a shilling per barrel, that is, for 54,000 barrels, a profit of £1,350 i.e. 33,750 frs.
    These figures are theoretical and indicate to you the maximum return that the kilns
    are capable of. Obviously we should not base our calculations on the maximum
    possible.

    Nevertheless, Mr Stack [9] assured Mr Duggan that he was guaranteed an annual demand
    of 30,000 barrels if he wished to re-open the kilns, which would give a profit of £750
    i.e. 18,750 frs. Mr Duggan and I think that it would be better to go below that figure to
    avoid disappointment and to calculate the annual profit from the lime kilns at £500
    i.e. 12,500 frs.

3   **Sawmill**
    I have already referred above to this source of revenue, but I have not yet got
    firm enough information to establish a figure which I can rely on.

---

[9] The vendor.

We should mention in passing that the estate has all the materials necessary for construction, building stones, lime, gravel, sand and that large quantities of these were sold in the past. Based on the documents which I have consulted, here is a summary of the financial situation you would arrive at by taking account only of the resources already existing:

1 Meadows and lands £500
2 Lime kilns   £500
3 Timber   £200
4 Creamery   £25

£1,225 i.e. 30,625 francs

The report above gives you a glimpse of the value of the Drishane estate independently of the buildings, farm, barns, stables etc which would not be productive because of the system of letting.

It would be a very bad calculation that would leave blank the splendid outbuildings, the stables built at great cost and with the latest modern finish, the yards which are vast and well converted for a poultry farm, especially since poultry farming is precisely the big industry in the country and the most remunerative. There is perfect and complete farm machinery in place that it would be regrettable to leave idle. All of this seems to point to the fact that you should run the estate yourselves rather than letting it to different parties. You would earn far greater revenue from it. Running it yourselves would allow you also to employ many local people (in the lime kilns, the saw mills and in the fields) who would appreciate the service you were providing. You have on your side an immense advantage. Mr Duggan is an expert of the first order in this area because it is in dairy and poultry farming that he has such a flourishing and rewarding business. He was given the task of publishing the official reports on this industry of which he is so knowledgeable; he is so devoted to you that he will manage your interests as well if not better than his own. Mr Duggan will be a valuable advisor to you as will Mrs Duggan who has a very developed and practical business sense. Here are the figures, according to their own experience, which will serve as a basis:

(a) Rearing large animals (cattle) for butchering will bring in per annum about £5 i.e. 125 frs per head.

(b) Milking cows or dairy cows will bring in (per annum) about £10 or 250 frs per head.

(c) Sheep will bring in £1 i.e. 25 frs per head, but with sheep a profit can be made in less than 6 months.

Poultry is also excellent, and with the water that you have in abundance in the form of lakes, ponds and river, ducks would also seem to be indicated.

A model farm would be one of the best industries you could possibly establish because the Drishane estate provides you with all the required facilities. You would in that way be of great help to the young women of the country to whom you would teach dairy and farming; and the industry in question would benefit everyone, others as well as yourselves.

(signed) C. Nain

The Lodge, Convent of the Holy
Drishane, Millstr

Clearly, on the basis of this analysis, the convent could be self-sufficient, indeed it could generate a substantial profit, from judicious exploitation of the lands and industries. Père Nain's advice – that the Sisters should run it themselves, not let it, as might have appeared the sensible decision at first sight – was taken. The Sisters set about running the entire estate from the moment of their arrival. Indeed, Mr Duggan had started implementing the plan before the arrival of the Sisters in Ireland.

THE PURCHASE

Once the decision was taken to purchase Drishane, the Sisters had to proceed quickly and efficiently on the business side of the purchase. However, negotiations were delicate because, simultaneously, they had to satisfy the ecclesiastical authorities as to what their purpose was in coming to Ireland and, specifically, to the Diocese of Kerry. The balance between those two sides was kept largely by Mr Duggan, acting on behalf of the Sisters. Of course, the fact that the Sisters were French-speaking, and that they were living in Paris, complicated the issue. Père Nain would appear to have functioned very well in English and he was a very valuable 'go-between' in the negotiations, acting as interpreter and translator of documents for the Sisters.

The actual date of purchase of Drishane is the 30th October 1908.

THIS INDENTURE made the thirtieth day of October one thousand nine hundred and eight between Patrick Stack of Ballinahown near Fermoy in the County of Cork Farmer of the one part and Sophie Henriette Deruelle, Eugenie Marie Delbecq, Germaine Gabrielle de Guibert and Thérèse Marie de Guibert all of number eight Abbé Grégoire Paris Spinsters (hereinafter collectively called the purchasers) of the other part. WHEREAS by deed poll bearing date the thirty-first day of July one thousand nine hundred and eight the Right and Honourable John Ross a judge of the Chancery Division of the High Court of Justice in Ireland under the authority of the "Landed Estates Court (Ireland) Act 1858" and of the acts amending the same for the consideration therein mentioned granted unto the said Patrick Stack the several hereditaments in said Deed-Poll particularly described inter alia ALL THAT part of the lands of Drishane More containing two hundred and seventy-three acres one rood and eight perches statute measure or thereabouts described in map to said Deed Poll annexed and situate in the Barony of West Muskerry and County of Cork bestowed unto the said Patrick Stack his heirs and assigns forever AND WHEREAS the said Patrick Stack has agreed with the purchasers for the sale to them of part of said hereditaments hereinafter particularly mentioned and described and intended to be hereby conveyed for the sum of nine thousand five hundred pounds NOW THIS INDENTURE WITNESSETH that in pursuance of said agreement and in consideration of the sum of nine thousand five hundred pounds paid to the said Patrick Stack by the purchasers at or previous to the execution of these presents out of monies belonging to them on a joint account the receipt whereof he doth hereby acknowledge the said Patrick Stack as beneficial owner doth hereby grant unto the said purchasers ALL THAT part of the lands of Drishane More containing two hundred and fifty acres statute measure or thereabouts and more particularly delineated and described in the map or plan endorsed on these presents color Red together with the mansion house offices and buildings erected or standing thereon with their appurtenances which said premises are situate in the Barony of Great Muskerry and County of Cork and are part of the said lands of Drishane More comprised in and conveyed by said Deed-Poll of the thirty-first day of July one thousand, nine hundred and eight bestowed unto and to the use of the purchasers their heirs and assigns forever as joint tenants in equity as well as at law AND said Patrick Stack hereby acknowledges the right of the purchasers to the production of said Deed-Poll of thirty-first day of July one thousand nine hundred and eight and hereby undertakes with the said purchasers for the safe custody of said Deed-Poll IN WITNESS whereof the parties hereto have hereunto set their hands and affixed their seals the day and year first therein WRITTEN -------------

Signed Sealed and Delivered by the said Patrick Stack
In presence of
Arthur Carroll, Solicitor Fermoy
Arthur Clarke, Solicitor Cork.[10]

---

[10] IJAD, Drishane Collection. Purchase Agreement, 30th October 1908.

MAP I

Part of the Lands of Dooneens
Drishane More & Lackabane
and
Parts of the Lands of Coole & Drominahilla

BARONY OF WEST MUSKERRY
Cº CORK

Scale Six Inches to One Statute Mile

ENLARGEMENTS
Five Feet Scale

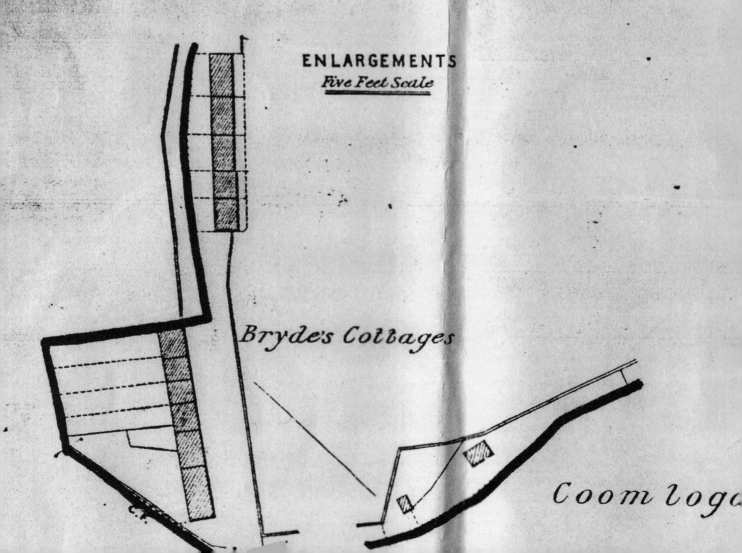

Bryde's Cottages

Coom logo

Drishane Beg

D O O N E E N S

C R.

Drishane Castle

Church
Burial Ground
EXCLUDED

C O O L

Quarry Yard

Creamery

Quarry Pit

Lime Kiln

D R I S H A N E M O R E

SATISFYING THE ECCLESIASTICAL AUTHORITIES

In several letters, Canon Casey, Parish Priest of Millstreet, to whom the Bishop delegated all diocesan dealings relating to the foundation, made it clear to the Sisters that they could not install themselves in Drishane, without the express permission of the ecclesiastical authorities. As late as December 1908, in a letter to Mr Duggan marked **Private**, he was still reiterating the power of the Church in the matter:

> I am afraid it is more than difficult for you to view this question from the standpoint of the Bishop. The Bishop looks on his receiving this Community into his diocese as a distinct concession on his part and he is anxious that the Nuns should have a clear understanding on this point. In your honest zeal and enthusiasm you appear to think that no others could work this quarry or get up any industries but this Community. You cannot perceive that their coming is any inconvenience to the Bishop of the Diocese or the Clergy of Millstreet[11]

The Sisters were involved in the purchase of a large property comprising a substantial farm as well as lime kilns and a timber business, which they proposed to run for the benefit of the people of the area, employing the men of the neighbourhood. They had also undertaken to open a school of housecraft and a knitting factory to provide training and employment for the women of the area. In the light of all those undertakings, and bearing in mind that it was in the first decade of the twentieth century when the people of Ireland had very little in the way of employment and virtually no education beyond the national school, it is hard to believe that the stumbling block in the negotiations with the ecclesiastical authorities was the provision of accommodation and an annual honorarium for a Chaplain. However, such was, indeed, the case.

In the original Programme[12] submitted for the approval of the Bishop, the Object of the Foundation was set out as being two-fold:

> 1 To secure a safe investment and home because of the harsh laws against religious in France;
>
> 2 To establish a novitiate and schools instead of those suppressed in Paris by the French Government, for training Continental, Irish and English ladies for teaching.

Under the heading, Proposed Industrial Works, three such works are listed:

> 1 The nuns shall start industrial works [...] such as carpet-making, domestic economy, embroidery, needlework, blouse-making etc. By doing so, they hope to enable the girls of the district to earn a decent living, and prevent them from going abroad.
>
> 2 They shall open limekilns, sawmills, etc. and exploit them to the fullest possible extent, employing local labour in those various industries.
>
> 3 They shall carry on and teach scientific farming – dairy work, poultry, either or both of them – but will not embark upon such works as are at present being carried on in the vicinity or in any way interfere with schools now established in the district.

---

[11] IJAD, Canon Casey to Mr Duggan, 3rd December 1908.
[12] IJAD, Père Nain Papers, 1908-1909. [Undated].

Before the arrival of the Sisters, Mrs Nora Duggan, writing to Mother St Marguerite Marie in Paris, reported:

> There is already sign of life. The lime is burning and being sold very quickly though only started some days. I am keeping for you the first coin received there, one shilling, and you will keep it as a souvenir.[13]

However, the section of the programme dealing with the Chaplain – effectively, that the Sisters would go to the parish church at first and then deal with the issue as it arose – was not acceptable to the Bishop. They had to draft a new section undertaking to pay a yearly salary to the chaplain. In order to guarantee that payment, they were required to invest a certain sum of money, the interest on which would make up the required salary. Lengthy negotiations were needed to reach an agreement, during which the requirements for settlement appear to become more costly. Within a month of the arrival of the first Sisters, the Canon acknowledged receipt of:

> Four Hundred Pounds, being the amount agreed upon with the Dames de St Maur to cover cost of alterations etc to Presbytery and other expenses incidental to introduction of Chaplain for their convent Drishane Castle.[14]

The original terms of agreement included the payment of an annual salary of £150 to the Chaplain.[15] Father O'Connor was duly appointed.

> The Chaplain is an excellent choice, very discreet, very prudent, and entirely devoted to our cause but alas, poor man!! He gets £7.10s a year for being Chaplain, all the rest goes to the Reverend CC. Of course he told us this as a great secret. He would not like it repeated … It is better for him to buy a little cow and we will give him grass for it – then perhaps he could sell it at the end of the year with a little profit.[16]

Sr St Beatrice had, on the advice of Père Nain, come home from Singapore to be the first Mistress of Novices. She was an extremely practical woman, so it is likely that she was serious when she suggested buying a cow. In a supremely ironic development, the Sisters, who were perceived as willing to spend large sums on developing the lands and not willing to spend a relatively small annual sum on a chaplain, supplemented the Chaplain's allowance (which they themselves were paying in accordance with the agreement reached with the diocese but which would not appear to have been passed on to him in full) from their own purse.

In addition to being a strategist, Père Nain appears to have been a consummate diplomat. He managed to bring the Bishop of Kerry, Dr Mangan, and the Parish Priest of Millstreet, Canon Casey, round to his way of thinking. Indeed, they became best friends with the Sisters and proved very supportive in the early days in Drishane.

---

[13] IJAD, Nora Duggan to Mother St Marguerite Marie, 2nd February 1909.
[14] IJAD, Canon Casey to Mr Duggan, 28th April 1909. Canon Casey here uses the name by which the Congregation was known in France; sometimes he refers in correspondence to 'your friends in Paris'.
[15] IJAD, Mr Duggan to Père Nain, 16th November 1908.
[16] IJAD, Sr St Beatrice to Mother St Marguerite Marie, 3rd August 1909. The initials CC probably stand for Canon Casey.

ESTABLISHMENT

ARRIVAL OF FIRST SISTERS

And so it was that on the 29th March 1909[17] the little contingent of just two Sisters arrived in Drishane, Mother St Marguerite Marie, Assistant General and Sr St Beatrice Foley, with her sister, Mrs Duggan. Mollie Duggan (Sr St Beatrice's niece), also came and stayed with the Sisters for a few days, proving extremely useful and helpful to them. On the 30th March another group of travellers arrived, Sr St Anthony, Sr Joseph (Bridget McCarthy, Tulla, County Clare) and Sr Geneviève (Augustine Rogues, Monchand, Haute Loire, France) all three from Weybridge community. On the 19th May, Mother St Claire Bringeon arrived from Weybridge, where she had been Superior for three years, to become Superior of Drishane. She was accompanied by Elisabeth (Rascoussier, Lozère, France) who remained in Drishane until her death in 1955. The Novitiate was set up in July, during the first visit of Mother St Henri, Superior General, who appointed Sr St Beatrice Foley as the first Mistress of Novices. So the two key sisters in the early years in Drishane were the Frenchwoman, Mother St Claire Bringeon, and the Irishwoman brought back from Singapore for the purpose, Mother St Beatrice Foley.

On the 25th May the first Mass was celebrated in the modest chapel, formerly the Wallis' dining-room.[18] It was decorated with paintings, candelabras and vases sent by the Communities of Toulouse, Montpellier, Nîmes and Cette (later known as Sète).

JEROME MACCARTHY, STEWARD

In all practical matters to do with the foundation in Drishane, Mr Duggan continued to be actively involved. One of his first tasks was to find a Steward; he found Jerome MacCarthy:

> How do you describe Jerome MacCarthy? He accepted with devotion, almost as a vocation, the task of looking after the interests of the new community and he didn't tell his family until he was leaving home. He started his apostolic work both on the farm and in the outbuildings. Everything had to be reorganised: the fields which had not been cultivated for several years, the kitchen garden, the terraces, the pleasure garden ... The house was home to mice and rats drawn by the Finnow stream which flows into the Blackwater.[19]

Whenever any issue arose in relation to Drishane, Canon Casey contacted Mr Duggan in order to keep him informed on developments:

> Just a line to say that I have just heard that Mick Looney and the Steward had some difference on Saturday and that Looney was dismissed from work. There was also a remark passed that the Steward was giving a preference to men from a neighbouring parish, had in fact dismissed some men from Millstreet and taken on some from the outside parish. Of course I know nothing of the merits of these statements. I only just listened.[20]

---

[17] IJAP, 6M 2-1 Drishane 1909-1967, 9-10.
[18] Ibid. Drishane Castle was the residence of the Wallis family for almost two hundred years before it became the property of Mr Stack.
[19] IJAD, report in *Drishane Convent Annals*, 1925.
[20] IJAD, Canon Casey to Mr Duggan, 26th April 1909.

The following day, Canon Casey had already discovered the truth of the matter which suggests that he acted rather too soon on what he had heard:

> I have just seen the Steward and learned that, as far as Looney is concerned, the report of last evening is entirely exaggerated. Looney is at work and there has been no difference of importance – only some matter that is to be referred to you for settlement.
> The Steward also told me that he had not dismissed the men, but only reduced the wages to 12 shillings, as much, he continued, as their work was value for.[21]

From the moment they arrived in Drishane, the Sisters set about establishing a centre of activity in north Cork at a time when employment was scarce if it was available at all, and when even those who had employment were really very poorly fed and housed. In the first thirty years of its existence, Drishane was employing over sixty workmen on the farm, in the saw mills, the lime kilns, the brush factory, and housing many of them; it was employing over thirty women in the knitting factory; it was supplying the boarders in both schools with nutritious food as well as supplementing the diet of the workers and their families. Indeed, some neighbours have commented that the workmen were paid as much again in kind as they were in cash, and that's why there were never any labour problems.[22] They include in their payment in kind, vegetables and other farm produce, as well as lime from the quarry for the soil as well as for their houses. So, from the very beginning, Drishane was embedded in the area and local families contributed to its growth and development.

DRISHANE'S FIRST REVEREND MOTHER

"It's our job to make the children happy; God will make them holy."

When Mother St Claire Bringeon was moved to Drishane as Mother Superior, there was a great sense of loss felt in Weybridge. She had been just three years there and by all accounts she was greatly loved. This proved to be the case in Drishane also. She had the ability to rise above all difficulties, to remain happy in the face of tremendous challenges and to keep everyone around her happy also. Her letters to the Mother House in Paris, and the accounts of her initiatives in the Drishane Annals reveal a warm, loving person. She can be mischievous, funny and even indiscreet, but she is always happy.

THE OPENING

Her first weeks and months in Drishane were dogged by The Opening, for which she always used the English words in her correspondence. She had been appointed Superior in Drishane in May. In July she received a visit from Mother General St Henri, her Assistant Mother St Marguerite Marie and Père Charles Nain. The Duggan family and Father Walsh[23] also came and meetings were held to plan various ventures, in particular, the Factory School, but also the question of an official opening.

---

[21] IJAD, Canon Casey to Mr Duggan, 27th April 1909.
[22] IJAD, Bertie Doody interview, RTE cassette tape, 1980s.
[23] Fr Dan Walsh was the uncle of Sr St James and Sr St Daniel Walsh and also of Sr St Albert and Sr St Elizabeth McSweeney; grand-uncle of Sr Hannah Murray now in Crawley.

In a letter to Mother St Marguerite Marie, now back in Paris, she complained that she was tired of The Opening.[24] She felt that too much importance was being attached to the ceremony. Father Walsh, who comes across as a wise man, advised her not to worry about it and to consider it as completely secondary to her various initiatives. She told Mother St Marguerite Marie that she had written an invitation to the Bishop of Kerry and had now decided in her own mind that, if he made a fuss, she would just cancel the whole thing. She would have the House blessed and leave it at that, or she would postpone it until the boarding school was opened. Mother St Beatrice also mentioned it in a letter to Paris in August 1909:

> Reverend Mother wrote to [the bishop] about the 'opening' a few days ago and is now waiting for a reply. Father O'Connor [bishop's secretary] says that he will put his foot down this time and make His Lordship take our date as his. We shall see!!![25]

Two days later Mother St Claire had a very gracious acceptance from the Bishop. Canon Casey, Parish Priest of Millstreet, was with her when the Bishop's response arrived and he was a bit put out. He was very keen to keep it simple and repeated that his idea was that there would be a private ceremony: the Bishop, the priests of the parish, and the Duggan family. There should be simply a blessing of the House now and a more elaborate ceremony and reception later for the priests and people of the surrounding area when there was more to show for their work in Drishane. Mother St Claire could hardly believe her ears. She was totally in agreement with the Canon, an occurrence so rare as to be remarkable. However, Mother St Marguerite Marie, one of the founders of Drishane, had expressed an interest in having a more elaborate ceremony and it was important to Mother St Claire to get her approval for any change to her preferred option. She also made the point that, if the Bishop was happy with the more low-key affair – and according to the Canon the Bishop would prefer it – then that made the decision easy for her because her main reason for having what she called the Grand Reception was that a more modest one would not sufficiently honour the Bishop.

The Annals for the year 1909 record that on the 8th September, the Feast of the Nativity of the Virgin Mary, there was a beautiful ceremony: the Blessing of the Chapel.[26] This was, however, no low-key affair. Under the heading 'Drishane Castle Blessed as Convent' the 'memorable ceremony' was reported in *The Cork Examiner* the following morning, Thursday, 9th September 1909, and was given many column inches, beginning

> Yesterday the Papal white and yellow floated proudly over the stately keep of Drishane Castle... The colours of the Papacy, replacing on the Castle flagstaff that which the people of the district had been wont to regard as the symbol of ascendancy, afforded the final proof that the transition was complete.[27]

The ceremony began at 11 a.m. with solemn High Mass. His Lordship Most Reverend Dr Mangan, Bishop of Kerry, presided. He was assisted by Very Reverend Canon Casey PP Millstreet. The celebrant was Reverend Father Fuller, Administrator, Killarney; the deacon, Reverend Father Huggard CC Millstreet; the sub-deacon, Reverend Father Cronin, Foreign

[24] IJAD, Mother St Claire to Mother St Marguerite Marie, 26th August 1909.
[25] IJAD, Mother St Beatrice to [Mother St Marguerite Marie], undated and incomplete. Content indicates that it is August 1909, after the 12th.
[26] IJAD, *Drishane Convent Annals*, 1909.
[27] *Cork Examiner*, 9th September 1909.

Missions, and the Master of Ceremonies was Reverend Father O'Connor, Killarney. In addition there were many more priests: Reverend Father White PP Dromtariffe; Reverend Dr Sexton, President Farranferris; Reverend Dr Scannell, Farranferris; Reverend Father O'Mahony CC St Patrick's; Reverend Father O'Brien CC; Reverend Father Ahern CC; Reverend Dr Daly, Athenry; Reverend Father Mulkerrin, London. There were also invited lay guests. It is hard to imagine how these fitted into the oratory of the time, which generations of past pupils will remember as the first classroom to the right of the main door.

Father Mulkerrin, in his homily, said that the mission of the Sisters in Ireland was a response to God's call as really and truly as Abraham's was. He exhorted the Sisters to think of the slums of the great cities in England, with which he was familiar, and the number of Irish girls that went over to England because there was no outlet for their talents or their industry in their own country.

The music of the Mass was rendered by a special choir from Cork, under the direction of Herr Theo Gmür. The Mass was Kempter's in D, opus 9. The proper of the Mass was Gregorian. Among the soloists mentioned is Miss Mollie Duggan, niece of Mother St Beatrice, Mistress of Novices, who sang the *Ave Maria* (Gmür) at the Offertory. The choir was made up of sopranos, Miss Mollie Duggan and Miss Eileen Gmür; altos, Mrs O'Connell, Miss Eileen Murphy, Miss Dennehy; tenors, Mr M Ambrose, Mr C F Fielding; basses Mr T Healy and Mr Howell.

After Mass, His Lordship and the guests were entertained to dinner by the community in the convent refectory. The catering was done by Leech's of Cork. The Bishop spoke after dinner and his words are also recorded in *The Cork Examiner:*

> Without going into the arguments that might be advanced as to the advantages of the multiplying of religious orders or not multiplying them, and speaking of the present religious order, His Lordship said that they had come over [to Ireland from France] for a unique purpose, and that was the teaching of industrial subjects. As Fr Mulkerrin had said in his sermon, he continued, they had no selfish motives whatsoever. They came purely to strive to educate and raise up the people, and it appeared to His Lordship, though he was speaking in the presence of gentlemen prominently connected with educational institutions, that one type of education was sadly wanted in this country. It had not been developed up to the present as it should have been developed, and that was industrial education. It would be useless, or almost useless, to transfer the soil of the country from the landlords to the people if the people were not instructed in how best to use the land. Unfortunately, for one reason or another in times past, they were not instructed in this respect, and even if they were they hadn't the incentive to work hard which was necessary to progress. There were obstacles in the way, but these obstacles were being rapidly removed, the Bishop continued (applause), and the people now had the incentive to work the land for all that it was worth, and all they were worth. He announced that this religious institution was founded in their midst, fortunately for Canon Casey and the surrounding country, for the chief - indeed the sole - purpose of instructing the people in how to keep their home. That was one of the reasons why His Lordship welcomed this religious institute. It would be unbecoming, he continued, if he didn't bid a hearty welcome to these good religious who had come amongst them (applause). They came from a land which in days past afforded a refuge to Irish people when they required a refuge. They came from a land in which their people and especially their priests got an education when education was denied them at home. His lordship regretted

> the reversal of this religious fervour in France which resulted in religious orders being driven out wholesale. It would be ungracious on the part of Ireland not to afford a refuge to those who were suffering for their religion in France. For that reason again he bid the order a very hearty welcome, and he trusted their work here would be as successful for the order itself as for the people amongst whom they were established. He hoped they would all live to celebrate the silver jubilee of the convent – he certainly hoped to be there himself – but if not he hoped that many of those now present would be made aware of the progress that had been made in the meantime and that the work done would be a blessed work, a useful work that would be good for Ireland.

These words of the Bishop of Kerry, Dr John Mangan, are interesting in the light of his adamant opposition to the foundation at Drishane throughout the negotiations of 1908. In a letter dated September 4th 1908 (a year earlier almost to the day), the Bishop's secretary responded on his behalf to Mother General in Paris:

> There is no room for a second convent at Millstreet except under very exceptional circumstances. The Community of Nuns at Millstreet are quite capable of supplying the educational wants of the district: moreover our communities find it very difficult to secure a sufficient supply of subjects at the present time. The convent at Millstreet and two other neighbouring convents have not got a subject for some ten years and more. Under these circumstances he thinks it is very undesirable to place another religious community in their midst, especially one which says its principal object in coming to Millstreet is to secure Irish subjects for foreign missions.[28]

All ensuing negotiations between the IJ Sisters and the ecclesiastical authorities stressed the farm, the school of housecraft and the knitting factory. On that basis, the Bishop was prepared to give the proposal due consideration:

> In order to be able to do so he wishes that your community in cooperation with the parish priest of Millstreet should agree to the terms on which you are to come to Millstreet, and that moreover a detailed scheme of the industrial work which you give an undertaking to carry on will be placed before him. When these particulars are placed before his Lordship, he will be prepared to give his views on the foundation, but cannot before then. His Lordship desires me to say that up to the time that this scheme is determined on, all correspondence must take place between you and the parish priest of Millstreet without reference to his Lordship.[29]

Even as late as January 1909, the Bishop was writing to Canon Casey:

> These Sisters are forcing themselves into this diocese where there is no want to be supplied by them. Kindly send a copy of this letter to the Sisters and to Mr Duggan.[30]

It was, therefore, very important that Fr Mulkerrin, in his homily at the official opening (effectively, speaking for the Sisters), would stress the founding of industries, specifically in order to keep Irish girls at home. It was also important, from the Bishop's point of view, that he would not appear to be in favour of an undertaking that he opposed so vigorously a matter of months earlier. He, therefore, presented the foundation he was blessing as quite a different thing from the one proposed in 1908. The aim of this foundation now was to run a model farm, in order to train the Irish people to tend the land which would soon be

---

[28] IJAD, Rev J O'Connor to Mother General St Henri, 4th September 1908.
[29] Ibid.
[30] IJAD, Bishop Mangan to Canon Casey copied in Canon Casey's hand, undated, but would appear to fit in with Canon Casey to Mr Duggan, 18th January 1909.

Verso in Père Nain's hand: six members of the Singapore Community including four Irish: Sr St Beatrice, Sr St Odon and Sr St Columba are pioneers.

Front L-R: Margaret Kelleher, Sr Aloysius, Mrs Pierce, Sr Ambrose;
Back L-R: Kathleen O'Connor, Eileen O'Sullivan, Bina Cronin, Josie O'Connor.

theirs; to teach the young women to look after their households; and to provide an outlet for the talent and industry of the female population of the surrounding area.

THE KNITTING SCHOOL

The Knitting School was set up in December 1909 with about twenty young women from Millstreet and the surrounding area, under the management and guidance of Sr St William (Georgina Mayes, London). It is always referred to in the Annals as The Factory School or The Knitting School. These names given to it by the founding Sisters show that the impetus was provided by the zeal of the Sisters to improve the lives of the women of the area through training and development. The skills which they acquired meant that they were then gainfully employed in a pleasant environment, which kept them in the area and gave them independent means of their own.

When the first twenty young women were recruited for the school, there really was nothing to indicate that Drishane was going to be a centre of industry. First of all there were no knitting machines. However, because the Sisters were keen to get going as soon as possible – and they could hardly have opened sooner than the year of their arrival – they took on the girls before the machines. But the young women were not idle for those first weeks. They were given classes in dress-making and also in cooking. These were extremely important skills and there was nowhere in the area that these skills could be acquired at that time.

THE INSPECTOR

'Notes on current issues'[31], an undated, unsigned document which would appear to have been written by Mother St Marguerite Marie to Mother St Claire, advises that a meeting should be arranged as soon as possible with Père Nain, Mr Duggan and the Inspector on the issue of the Factory School. The main item on the agenda should be the choice of machines. The Inspector's input is urgently required on this issue and also on the question of an electric motor for the machines. In a letter from Mother St Claire to Mother St Marguerite Marie an account of the Inspector's visit is given.[32]

The day started with the arrival of Mr Duggan at 10 a.m. 'The Inspector is coming!' he announced, and added that he had also warned Canon Casey. Poor Mother St Claire was beside herself. She realized that Mr Duggan's intentions were good, but she would have preferred to have dealt with the Inspector without the Canon.

So they all sat, and waited, the Canon, Mr Duggan and Mother St Claire. Time passed. Lunch-time came and they shared the convent lunch with Mr Duggan. The poor Canon had to leave without meeting the Inspector. Mr Duggan left later. Night fell. No Inspector.

The following morning, when the Canon came to say Mass, he brought a telegram from the Inspector, explaining that he had failed to alight at Millstreet station and had continued

---

[31] IJAD, Drishane Collection [undated and unsigned].
[32] IJAD, Mother St Claire to Mother St Marguerite Marie, 28th August 1909.

on to Killarney. However, he promised to visit Drishane on the return journey at 8.30 a.m. Once again they waited and once again the Inspector failed to materialize. The Canon left in despair, advising the Sisters to send the Inspector on to him if he came – which he did, just a quarter of an hour after the Canon had left. Mother St Claire was delighted. They could have their meeting without interruption.

The Inspector was completely satisfied with their plans for the factory. He had no idea that they had such detailed written plans for the project and displayed a lively interest in them and read them attentively. He promised that he would get catalogues for the machines which would be best suited to their needs and that the manufacturers would send someone to train them in their use. He also undertook to find a suitable person to oversee the factory school. The ideal would be someone with experience rather than someone with qualifications. He was afraid that he would not find a Catholic. The Sisters assured him that, while they would have a preference for a Catholic, it didn't matter if none could be found. He intended to enlist the help of the machine manufacturers in that also. As he was not very well informed, he promised to put the Sisters in touch with a department inspector who would be. Finally, he would get them a refund of three-quarters of what they had spent and a grant towards the training of the young women. He was most impressed with the rooms, which were filled with light.

As soon as the machines arrived, training in their use began. The girls learned very quickly, so much so that they surprised Mother General and Mother St Marguerite Marie during their visit from Paris the following year with their familiarity with the machines and their skill in handling them. The girls were able to demonstrate their ability to make different little useful items. And their training was not confined to mechanical matters. When the two Mothers paid another visit the following year, one of the girls, on behalf of all of them, made a delightful speech of welcome in French. They were all granted a free day and also invited to take part in the Procession of the Blessed Sacrament along with the Community, children from Millstreet and Drishane pupils. On subsequent visits, they sang for Mother General.

'THE STRIKE'

In the year 1917 the Annals record that something happened in the knitting school. The pupils sent a written request to Reverend Mother for a wage increase and awaited her reply. On the morning of the 12th February, instead of starting their work as usual, they pronounced themselves On Strike and remained motionless at their machines. Fortunately, the strike was short-lived. Reverend Mother explained to them that their request was unreasonable. They were paid not by the day but by the piece, with the result that, if they came late – as many of them did – they did not complete many pieces, and thereby reduced their pay. She suggested to them that they should consider coming earlier in the morning. They would then complete more garments and get what they wanted – more pay. By mid-day they were all working away at their machines.

PLAN FOR A PUMP [33]

This note is written on a detailed drawing for a pump to be installed in order to improve access to the lime in the quarry. Lime made an important contribution to the income in Drishane in the early years and Mother St Claire is concerned that the source of supply is seriously depleted. She is writing about it to 'Mother General' but, because it is undated, it is not possible to say which one. However, it is probably safe to assume that it is addressed to Mother St Marguerite Marie who, as Assistant Mother General, was very involved in the founding of Drishane, and retained a close interest in every detail of developments there throughout her period in office as Mother General.

1   The pump with its electric motor (230 volts), its regulator etc. – its tubing for suction and contra-flow with instruments to attach it or to move it.

2   Galvanised iron pipes joining up A the actual quarry with the quarry lake; B the quarry lake with the turbine lake.

3   Electric cable between the pump motor and the trolley dynamo. This pump can empty 200 gallons of water per minute, and has a depth of 15 feet (4m.50). The quarry lake has a depth of 9 or 10 feet – its level (when full of water) is already a little below that of the actual quarry.

Plan: To empty the water from the quarry lake, and in that way empty the quarry itself; **dig the quarry** to a depth of 8 or 9 feet; **then dig the lake** to a depth of 15 feet etc. The stone is certainly very good.

Mr Hennessy has raised to £114.10 the price for installing this pump, all found, except for the **cement** for the platform on which the pump and its motor will sit, and also, our men's help and the **small building** which will house the said pump.

Jerome has spoken to Mr Hennessy about this new estimate ... and Mr Hennessy is dealing with it. He said, "I've given the highest price that it could be, but I hope that it will come in lower, depending on whether the terrain requires more or less piping."

The pump itself costs £61 of the £114. Jerome's costs £35 or £40.
At the very start we had to choose between that pump at £61, being worked by our engine, and another pump at £104, being worked by a petrol machine. The advantage of the latter is its independence of the engine, so the cost of installing it is less. When examined closely, the costs are not enormous, just £3 to connect the pump and the engine. And these costs will quickly be compensated by the lower fuel costs, leaving aside the difference in price between the two pumps.

Mr Hennessy has not yet replied, but I'm not waiting for his reply before submitting this to you, Ma Très Honorée Mère, because given the impossibility of extracting more from the quarry, we really have to install this pump before the Spring. The little corner of the quarry which we can still extract is much smaller than I had realised, now that I can see it cleaned.

---

[33] IJAP, 6M 2-3, drawing showing plan for a pump with explanation in Mother St Claire's hand addressed to Mother General [undated].

Projet Pompe.

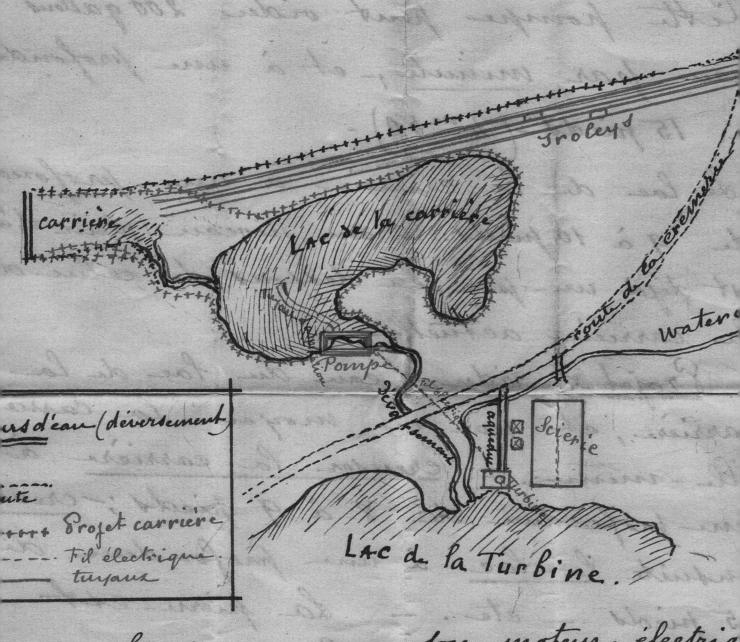

carrière

Troleys

Lac de la carrière

route de la Crémerie

water

Pompe

cours d'eau (déversement

aqueduc

Scierie

Projet carrière

Fil électrique
tuyaux

Lac de la Turbine.

1º. La pompe avec son moteur électriq
son régulateur, etc. — ses tuyaux refoul
aspirants avec instruments pour les fixer
déplacer. —

2º. Tuyaux en fer galvanisé mettant
communication A la carrière actuelle ave
lac de la carrière ; — B le lac de la carriè
le lac de la Turbine.

The Sisters, ever loyal to their young women, felt that the incident occurred because of outside influence. In any event, nothing came of it. They seemed to be very happy with their lot and to benefit greatly from their time in Drishane. They featured in every visit of Mother General and were an important group in the life of the house. For instance, in 1925, when Fr Mulkerrin gave the Retreat, those attending included twenty-five from the factory school and about thirty past-pupils.

THE CHRISTMAS TREE

From the arrival of the Sisters in 1909 until the Silver Jubilee in 1934 the story recorded in the Drishane Annals, always hand-written in French, is very much a story of growth and change. One of the annual events, which became an established tradition and a fixture on the calendar, is referred to in the Annals using the English words, 'The Christmas Tree'.[34]

The Christmas Tree is first mentioned in 1910 as a surprise for the pupils of The Knitting School. (The boarding school and the domestic economy school had not yet opened.) There were about twenty young women there at the start. Each of them was told that she could bring in her little brothers and sisters on December 27th. About eighty children gathered in the recreation hall which was hardly big enough to accommodate them. Toys, which had been placed on the tree, were distributed to the children. Then they had tea and cakes. Everyone went home with a gift of an item of clothing, presented by Mother St Claire.

At Christmas 1912, Mother St Marguerite Marie, Assistant General and one of the founders of Drishane, was on a return visit, so she presided over the ceremony. By 1913 the Community had grown to twenty-five Sisters. The Christmas Tree was bigger and better than in previous years and the large room could barely hold the crowd. The grown-ups had chairs or benches to sit on; the little ones had the floor, where they made a pretty picture, sitting in circles, admiring each other's gifts. By now the boarding school had been in operation for two years and two boarders, who had not gone home for the holidays, distributed cakes and served tea to the whole gathering.

By 1914, construction of the new Domestic Economy School was completed, and the school was opened in October with twelve pupils. The domestic economy school provided ample space for the annual gathering and The Christmas Tree was erected in its largest room. A baby Jesus in his crib was placed close to the tree. It was the year of the outbreak of World War I and all present addressed a fervent prayer to Him for peace in the world. The tree was magnificent, covered in toys and sparkling with lights. Reverend Mother distributed gifts of warm clothes. After tea the young women of the factory school showed their gratitude by performing songs and dances for the Community. In 1915, the second Christmas of the War, prayers of thanksgiving were said for the Sisters in Belgium who had been saved. What is described as a hurricane raged right through Christmas in Drishane, nevertheless the tradition of The Christmas Tree was not broken.

---

[34] IJAD, *Drishane Convent Annals* 1910–1932.

In 1916, prayers continued for past pupils and families in France affected by the War and for those in Ireland affected by the Rising and its aftermath. But, for the little ones, Christmas and The Christmas Tree were the same as ever. That year there were one hundred and ten children who were given their gifts of toys and warm clothes by Mother St Beatrice, Mistress of Novices, as Reverend Mother – and indeed many in the Community – were in bed with 'flu. Unbelievably, the War still raged in 1917 and prayers were said that this would be the last Christmas of the War.

Two years after the end of World War I, in 1920, the Sisters were wondering, once again, whether they should have the traditional Christmas Tree, this time because there was such turmoil in Ireland due to the War of Independence. However, they concluded that these poor Irish children had so little joy in their lives that they should go ahead with the traditional celebration. A few days before Christmas 1921 peace terms were published and the omens were good for an end to hostilities.

Mother St Claire was Reverend Mother from 1909 to 1926. She spent Christmas 1925 in Paris but the tradition was carried on in her absence and the numbers were the greatest yet: 250 presents were distributed. The Christmas Tree tradition was kept up after her departure under her successor Mother St Etienne Flahault. By 1928 the numbers attending had risen to 350. Every one of the children, even the bigger ones, left with their hands full of useful presents, clothes and pious objects, after tea served by the novices. The following year, 1929, the numbers rose to 400. In December 1932, however, diphtheria was raging in the area. Nobody in Drishane was affected, but The Christmas Tree was cancelled.

1913 School Portrait
Back L-R: Hannah Fitzgerald (Sr St Thomas); Eileen Enright (Sr St Patrick); Kitty Fitzgerald (Sr St Aidan);
Miss O'Mullane (Sr St Kieran); Miss O'Connell; Nora Whelan; Maisie Clarke; Sheila Clarke (Sr St Patricia);
Front L-R: Eileen Clarke; Lily Johnson; Thérèse Tabouillot; Patricia Walsh (Sr St James); Patsy McCarthy.

THE BOARDING SCHOOL

In October of 1911 the boarding school was opened with five pupils. The first Head Mistress was Sr St Mary Magdalen Foley, sister of Mother St Beatrice. Sent from Wolverhampton for the purpose, unfortunately she could not stay, and left for France almost as soon as she had arrived.[35] The Drishane Convent Annals record that she was replaced a few weeks later (on the eve of celebrating Christmas). However, the name of her successor is not recorded. In any event, with five pupils it is likely that the task of Head Mistress was not an onerous one at the beginning and that the role was held jointly with that of Superior. The following year eight pupils were mentioned, including two French girls, one of whom was the niece of Abbé Descamps of Lille, who knew the congregation very well in France. The pupils would appear to be of varying ages in the early years, because three were presented for Matriculation for the first time in 1914: all three were successful. That year also, Patricia Walsh (Mother St Beatrice's niece) was chosen, as the eldest pupil, to welcome Mother General.

It is remarkable how soon after the founding of Drishane past pupils and their sisters and cousins start to enter the Novitiate: Mary Wickham, one of the first pupils, entered in 1914 and, as Sr St Stanislaus (Sligo), was to serve as Superior of Drishane from 1950-1958 and, subsequently, as the first Provincial Superior of England and Ireland. Her niece, also Mary Wickham from Sligo, entered in 1935 and became Sr St Celestine, a gifted artist and teacher. She was followed into the Novitiate in 1954 by her cousin, Pauline O'Dwyer from Dublin who served throughout the Province, and in California for many years. Patricia Walsh also entered the Novitiate in 1914 and, after her first profession in 1916, went out to Japan as Sr St James (Cork city). Her sister, Eily, entered the following year and, as Sr St Daniel, went to Singapore in 1919. During the same visit Mother General did the honours when Miss Eileen Enright was elected the first President of the Legion of Mary. She became Mother St Patrick (Pallaskenry, Co. Limerick), serving as Mother St Beatrice's successor as Mistress of Novices and going on to found Rosslyn House in Weybridge in 1950.

In September 1914 the boarders were nineteen in number; by 1927 that number had risen to almost seventy. In April 1927 a national pilgrimage was organized to take the girls from the boarding schools of Ireland to Lourdes. Drishane formed a group of almost a hundred, including the eight teachers accompanying the pupils, both past and present.[36]

PLAYS, CONCERTS AND MUSICALS

From the earliest days of the boarding school and also of the school of housecraft, every celebration included a performance by the pupils. A feature of the programming was that there were four plays: one in English, one in French, one in Latin and one in Irish. Dr Browne, Professor in Maynooth, translated the classical tragedies into Irish for these performances by the girls.

---

[35] IJAP, 6M 2-1 Drishane 1909-1967, 14.
[36] IJAD, *Drishane Convent Annals*, 1927.

Welcome à Notre Très Honorée Mère

et à Révérende Mère Sainte Claire

Brisbane... 23 Juin 1927

Hymne à Sainte Marguerite - Marie.

Le Poème de la Maison.

Maison   Miss Isolda Peterson

Chant : Ma Maison . G. Nadaud

Porte   Miss Rosie Lawton

Cheminée   Miss Ethel Prendergast

Chanson du Vent { L. Mercier   Miss Sheila Barrett
                 { Prof. Gmür

Chapelle   Miss Betty Cahill

Violon : Le Ciel a visité la Terre . Gounod. Miss Bridget Mac Carthy

La Table   Miss Geneviève Flahault

La Cloche   Miss Maureen Moriarty

Piano : Les Cloches du Monastère

La Rivière et le Lac   { Miss Maureen O'Connor
                           { Miss Kathleen O'Flaherty

Les Champs et les Prés   { Miss Nuala Healy
                           { Miss Madeleine O'Connor

Chœur : Gai Rossignol H. Colas.

Opposite: Programme for entertainment provided for Mother General St Marguerite-Marie and Mother St Claire when they returned on a visit to Drishane in 1927

Above: The Irish Press Report of the performance by Drishane pupils of "Iphigenia" translated into Irish by Dr Paddy Browne

School of Housecraft: Sr St Paul O'Flynn
instructs her pupils in poultry farming

> It is owing to the enterprise and generosity of three outstanding religious: Mother Eucharia in Loreto Hall, Saint Stephen's Green, Mother Clement in the Dominican Convent, Eccles Street, and Madame Saint Etienne in the Drishane Convent in Millstreet, in Cork, that my Uncle Paddy's life's work – his translations of the classical theatre of Europe and the ancient world – did not sink, unperformed, without trace.[37]

A highlight of this practice was in 1931 when the girls travelled to Cork to perform *Athalie* in UCC.[38] At 11.30 am a special train took 130 (Sisters and pupils) from Millstreet to Cork where they proceeded on foot to the university. A splendid welcome awaited them there, with floral arrangements on the tables for a beautifully served lunch. The President of the University facilitated them in this, as well as by allowing them to transform the *aula maxima* into a theatre, with sets representing the vestibule of the temple. At 5 pm the curtain rose to a crowded auditorium and the attention of the audience was gripped from the first scene. Athalie was played by Eileen McElligott who, although only sixteen years of age, managed to look fifty; she was dressed in black and gold, with a red velvet cloak, a veil and a gleaming tiara. She played the part to perfection. Eileen McElligott, as Mother Eucharia, went on to become Mother General of the Columban Sisters while her sister, Elizabeth, became Sr St Mary Philomena (Castleisland, Co. Kerry) who was the driving force in the knitting factory in Ballyferriter for almost thirty years.

The choir was accompanied by Sr St Kevin (Kathleen Dowling, Linkardstown, Co. Carlow) who, according to this account, 'passed the soul of Mendelssohn through her fingers'. The High Priest with his tiara and his two tunics, the outer one made of scarlet silk, was played convincingly by Sheila O'Donoghue. Sheila's uncle was Professor Tadhg O'Donoghue (UCC: 1916-1944), renowned Irish scholar, who wrote under the pen-name Torna. It was generally agreed that the entire cast had honoured Racine, his translator Dr Browne, and their school Drishane. Professor O'Donoghue and Dr Browne both spoke after the performance, and then supper was served. Finally, as well as the happy memories, the pleasure given by the performance, and the wonderful day out, the record shows that £50 was raised for the building of the new chapel.

THE SCHOOL OF HOUSECRAFT

In the month of June 1913 work began on the foundations of the new building which would be the School of Housecraft. Mother St Marguerite Marie had by now succeeded Mother St Henri as Mother General, and when she visited the following summer she was keen to inspect the building. It was by then complete and the interior work was already well advanced.[39] It was opened at the end of October 1914 with twelve pupils. Sr St Gabriel (Bridget Galvin, Toureen, Ennis, Co. Clare) was brought back from Weybridge to take charge of it. Two qualified secular teachers were also appointed. Sr St Paul (Margaret Barnwell, Askeaton, Co. Limerick) who was professed in 1915 assisted in this school for young women, who were not admitted under the age of sixteen years. The Bishop visited and expressed his satisfaction with the school. He said Mass the following morning, during which the children sang in English and in Latin. The school grew faster than the boarding school, and already had thirty-one enrolled in its second year. This shows its success, as the

---

37 Máire Cruise O'Brien, *The Same Age as the State* (Dublin: O'Brien Press, 2003), 99.
38 IJAP, 6M 2-1 Drishane 1909-1967, 135.
39 IJAD, *Drishane Convent Annals*, 1914.

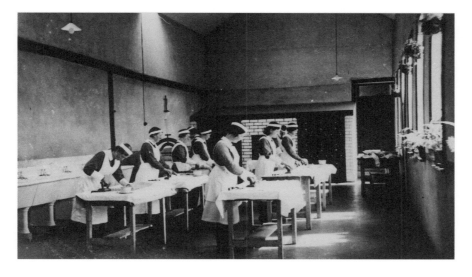

Above: Domestic School Farm Work
Below: Domestic School Ironing

course is just a year long, so a new group must be recruited each year. Indeed, at the end of the third year, the Annals record disappointment that only four or five out of thirty-two are 'considering returning', that is, to the Novitiate. The two schools worked closely together in the early years and both were involved in the various productions: the musical, *Maritana,* and *Grammar,* a work by the French comic writer Labiche were mentioned in 1920. In 1927, the boarders performed *The Roses of St Dorothy* while the School of Housecraft pupils enacted the parts played by all the different elements in Drishane in *The Poem of the House.* Another practice which was common to the Boarding School and the School of Housecraft was that of enrolling French girls as pupils.

HISTORICAL EVENTS

It is remarkable when following in the Annals the day-to-day lives of the Sisters in Drishane that they are always conscious of events in the wider world. This is particularly poignant in times of war, when they were praying for their Sisters in the countries most affected. So, early in 1918 for instance, they were reading long letters from Lille, Roubaix and Valenciennes, in which their Sisters described their lives under the German occupation.[40] In April of the same year, the Annals record great agitation in the country when the British government announced its intention to extend conscription to Ireland, followed by profound consolation when the Irish bishops opposed the move. Conscription was not introduced.

From the very beginning, the key employee in Drishane was Jerome MacCarthy, the steward on the farm. He was referred to by the Sisters as their 'treasure'; they trusted him and relied on him totally. It was, therefore, a great blow to the Drishane family when, on the 2nd December 1920, he was arrested and imprisoned.

1921 was an eventful year for Drishane. On the 1st April the railway bridge near the lodge was burned, so no train and, therefore, no post could get through. The Sisters were concerned as to how the pupils would get back to school.

VISITS TO DRISHANE BY THE CROWN FORCES [41]

Towards the end of April 1921 English soldiers visited Drishane for the first time. They suddenly appeared on the back avenue and proceeded down the terraces. The soldiers halted and the officer, alone, came to ring at the convent door. He asked for Reverend Mother and excused himself for having entered the property. He had taken the French flag which was flying from the top of the tower for an Irish flag. He also enquired whether the buildings belonged to the Sisters. On being answered in the affirmative he left, excusing himself once more for having brought his men on to their terrain. They came twice more, but in small numbers, looking for bread and vegetables.

---

[40] IJAP, 6M 2-1 Drishane 1909-1967.
[41] Ibid. For the most part, the Drishane register held in the Paris archive mirrors the Drishane Annals held in Dublin. An exception is the section under this heading, dealing with 1921 and 1922, where the register and Mother St Claire's letters to Mother St Marguerite Marie held in Paris provide valuable historical details. This section is based entirely on that material.

The Sisters kept up correspondence with Jerome in prison, and continued to take his advice on matters to do with the farm. In May, Mother St Claire reported that the Black and Tans were still around. They killed two men who failed to stop when they called out. She added that she had received a long letter from Jerome. He was worried about the saw-mills and asked her to tell the men to work hard:

> If some of us in here had the good fortune to be in their place now, we wouldn't complain if we had to work fourteen hours a day.[42]

On the 11th May towards 10 o'clock English troops invaded Drishane lands from all points simultaneously. In a few minutes there were two hundred soldiers in the fields and the gardens surrounding the house. They rounded up the workers and took eight of them to Millstreet for questioning. The search continued and at 1.15 they were on the point of taking all the men from the saw-mills when Reverend Mother protested to the officer who, it seemed, was not comfortable with the orders he had been given. He promised to send back the men very quickly. They were all home by evening, apart from three who were detained for a fortnight.

On the 12th May at seven o'clock in the evening the military and police came again, but this time they concentrated on the farm. They were led by the same officer who a fortnight earlier had apologised for being on convent property. Mother St Claire pointed this out to him; he apologised again and gave orders to his men to leave.

On the 14th May at 5.30 in the morning, they were there again. As on the 12th they surrounded the farm and started to search the stables and the workmen's rooms. Mother St Claire got dressed quickly and ran to the farm. The officer this time said he had orders to arrest a man whom he did not name. He pointed out that he had to obey orders. Mother St Claire replied that the manner in which he obeyed them was up to him. In England he would not behave like this, she added. He suggested that she should write to his General and, even though she didn't have great confidence in the outcome, she did send a telegram to the General. He replied by telegram that evening, expressing regret at the intrusion and informing her that he had given orders that it should not happen again. When about 300 Black and Tans or 'Auxiliaries' came to replace the soldiers in Millstreet, Mother St Claire expressed the hope that the telegram from the General would be honoured by these new troops, who were much more terrible than those before.

For six weeks they stayed away. On Monday 27th June at 2 o'clock in the afternoon, two cars arrived and a crowd of soldiers. The cars stopped at the foot of the tower and the troops surrounded the castle, but they did not go inside, except for two soldiers who entered the laundry, where they found an Irish sister. They asked her if she was French and on hearing the reply in the negative, one of them pretended he wanted to kill her. Meanwhile, the officer had rung the bell at the main door and presented this letter to Reverend Mother.

---

[42] IJAP, cited in Mother St Claire to Mother General, 9th May 1921.

RÉPUBLIQUE FRANÇAISE.

TÉLÉGRAMME

= MERE STEMMANUEL 8

GREGOIRE PAR

L'État n'est soumis à aucune responsabilité à raison du service de télégraphique. (Loi du 29 novembre 1850, art. 6.)

	NUMÉRO.	NOMBRE DE MOTS.	DATE.	
TREET	05328	12	10	M

JEROME LIBERE ARRIVE C

POSTES ET TÉLÉGRAPHES.

E LABBE

re
ols
est

N° ....

Timbre
à date.

BOURSE
10
21 12
PA

espondance privée par la voie

ÔT.

MENTIONS DE SERVICE.

MATIN =

Staff Headquarters
Buttevant
23.6.1921
Madame
Having been informed that wounded rebels had been taken into your convent, I have
given orders that only 'women searchers' enter the part of the convent inhabited by women.
I rely on you to do what you can to help these women to carry out my orders.
With good wishes,

(signed) E H Willis
Colonel Commanding the Kerry Brigade

Having presented that letter, the officer brought the 'women searchers' in. Mother St Claire protested, of course, but thought that in order to avoid worse, it was better to facilitate things. She had heard about a Jesuit college in Dublin where everyone was locked in the chapel, while the house was searched by the soldiers. So she watched, helpless, meditating on the contrast between the calm and peace of Drishane (at that moment looking particularly beautiful because of the glorious summer) and the 'repugnant hordes' spreading out over the grounds. Even the 'women searchers' noticed the contrast: 'How peaceful it is here' one of them said to her. But when Mother St Claire saw her workers standing so tall, so noble in their ragged clothes, under guard at the foot of the tower, she was convinced that the power of brute force is really quite limited.

So, while she calmly led one woman to the ground floor, another Sister led another to the first floor and two Sisters went to the upper floor with the third woman. The three women, although they did a thorough search, were not aggressive. The visit lasted three hours. Before leaving they made the community and the children pass through the parlour three by three in order to search their pockets and ensure that they were not carrying anything suspicious.

When they were leaving the officer asked Reverend Mother to sign a paper to attest that no damage had been done in the house. The document was signed. The searchers had damaged nothing, broken nothing, taken nothing. The account ends:

> Elles n'avaient fait que ... la chose la plus révoltante pour des personnes honnêtes et ayant un peu de dignité ... les fouiller.[43]

The account notes that at the start of July, England asked for an armistice; Dáil Eireann, the Irish parliament, met and opted also for the armistice. At the meeting in London the following December, one of the first conditions was the return of the prisoners to their families. At that news there was great rejoicing in the whole of Ireland but especially in Drishane, as it meant that their 'dear and devoted steward' would be back. The whole Drishane family, community and pupils, was overjoyed. Three days later, there was a big celebration in his honour, to which Irish officers, Mr MacCarthy's companions in captivity, and all the Drishane personnel were invited. The programme was specially devised for the occasion, and included plays, interval acts, singing, all in Irish. The first play performed was *Íosagán,* written by Patrick Pearse.

---

[43] They had only done ... the most revolting thing they could to honest and dignified people ... they had searched them.

At the celebrations, which were a real triumph, the only regret was the absence of their dear Reverend Mother Saint Claire, who was accompanying Mother General on her visit to the Far East. Her sympathy for the Irish cause was well known and they wanted her included now in the celebrations, so they sent her a radio-telegram.

Jerome MacCarthy continued in the employment of the Sisters in Drishane until 1933, when the Annals report that, on the 8th December, he and his family left Drishane for good. By this time their industry having closed down, the Sisters' activity was concentrated on the Schools, and a steward was no longer necessary. However, they remained grateful to him for all he had done for them over twenty-five years.

Sr St Mary Magdalen (Kathleen McGillycuddy, Killorglin, Co. Kerry) was professed in 1934 and spent her entire life in Drishane, until her death in 1990. Not only did she run the farm, but she also took on responsibility for all the plant and equipment in Drishane. Anything that required attention, whether it was a plumbing problem, an electrical problem, or any other problem in between, it was Sr St Mary Magdalen who was called on. She solved everything, with the help and support of the men who worked in Drishane and who had enormous respect for her, because of her great energy and her kindness to them and to everyone she met.

Above L-R: Jerome MacCarthy; Dandy;
Pat Quinn; Home Rule; Michael O'Reilly.   Below: Sr St Mary Magdalen

DEATHS OF PÈRE CHARLES NAIN AND MÈRE ST HOMBELINE

There was great joy in Drishane in May 1914 when Père Charles Nain came on a visit. He was delighted to be back also. However, after a fortnight he was recalled to France by telegram; his mother was seriously ill. He left immediately, promising to return before the end of the year and indicating that he would certainly be back before he set out again for Singapore. Unfortunately, due to the outbreak of World War I in August of that year, he was never to return to his beloved Drishane. He died on the 28th June 1916.

His brother, who was Parish Priest of Romenay (Saône et Loire) wrote to Drishane giving details of the final weeks of his life.[44] He was unwell at the beginning of May, but was confident that he would recover by following carefully his doctor's instructions as regards diet. However, as the month progressed he became increasingly weak. At this time he was in Dijon military hospital. The military authorities, thinking that the Vichy waters would do him good, sent him there by train on the 24th June and treated him with great care. A special compartment was reserved for him; a military nurse/priest accompanied him and, when the train stopped at a station, a soldier stood guard in front of his carriage so that he would not be disturbed.

On Wednesday, the 28th June 1916 at 2 o'clock in the afternoon his brother received a telegram announcing his death. He describes how his brother was laid out in a little room transformed into a chapel. He was surrounded by six soldier priests and members of the Red Cross. On the 30th June, Feast of the Sacred Heart, in the Church of St Blaise in Vichy, a very imposing funeral service took place with sung High Requiem Mass. His surplice and stole lay on his coffin as well as magnificent wreaths, one crossed with the tricolour which carried the inscription: *Mort pour Dieu et la Patrie*. About twenty officers were in the front row; behind them were more than a hundred war-wounded. An enormous crowd filled the church. Afterwards, as the cortège moved through the town, everyone, whether civilian or military, doffed his hat at its passing. Having arrived in the cemetery, the corpse was placed provisionally in a tomb. On the 5th July, the coffin left Vichy and, on the following day, was placed in the family vault in Farges-les-Mâcon.

Later that year, on the 9th November, the Annals record the death of Mother St Hombeline, Superior of Singapore, 'best benefactor'. She it was who, at the request of Père Nain, had generously given Mother St Beatrice to Drishane to start the Novitiate in 1909. These two deaths are linked in the Annals where the view is expressed that, while Mother St Hombeline and Père Nain might not have seen the fruits of their labours on this earth – although fifteen Drishane professed had already left for the Missions of Malaya and Japan – nevertheless, they will continue as the Protectors of their Irish foundation and the growth in vocations for the Missions will come:

> If it please God, this mustard seed will grow into a great tree with its branches spread out where the birds of the air will come to rest.[45]

---

[44] IJAD, *Drishane Convent Annals*, 1916(1).
[45] IJAD, *Drishane Convent Annals*, 1916(2).

BALLYFERRITER

HOLIDAYS IN KERRY

The Drishane Sisters' first experience of a holiday in West Kerry was in 1928. In the first three months of that year, a severe 'flu epidemic struck the community. Dr Paddy Browne, who translated the European classic theatre into Irish, offered his bungalow in Dunquin, where the Sisters could benefit from the sea air and build up their strength to continue their work until the end of the academic year. They went in groups over the Easter break. That holiday was judged to have been such a success that Mother General gave them permission to rent a house in Ballinskelligs in July. That was a sizeable house and could accommodate fourteen people. It had the added benefit of having its own chapel. In 1931, in a letter whose main purpose was to thank Mother St Etienne for her kind gift to him following the staging by Drishane pupils of his translation of *Athalie,* Dr Browne wrote inviting the Sisters again:

> I wrote yesterday to Brighid, and I hope that she will have everything ready. The time is short, and I hope that the visitors will stay as long as possible, that is to say, until the actual Wednesday of Holy Week. I leave Dunquin on the Sunday after Easter, and the house will be free for you from then until the 20th May.[46]

By the following summer, a bungalow had been built in St John's Wood in Millstreet. The Sisters spent their holidays in Drishane and went on outings to the bungalow, which was equipped with cooking facilities, so they could spend all day there. By the summer of 1933 the bungalow had been upgraded and could now accommodate about a dozen Sisters at a time, so they went there in turns throughout the months of July and August for the next two summers. Then, in September 1934, permission was given by Mother General and the Council to buy a plot of land in Ballyferriter to build a bungalow. The site was chosen in an ideal location, between the sea and the mountain called Cruach Mháirtín. The house, which the Sisters named Tigh Ioseph, was opened in 1935 as a holiday home for Drishane.

THE KNITTING FACTORY

The following year the knitting factory, which was making such a valuable contribution to the social and economic well-being of the women of the area around Drishane, was extended to Ballyferriter. Sr St Martin (Helena Fitzgerald, Kilbrittain, Co. Cork), Sr St Mary Philomena, Sr Finbar (Mollie Murphy, Millstreet, Co. Cork) and Sr Philomena (Mary Riordan, Ballyvourney, Co. Cork) moved there from Drishane. Kitty Forde, a young woman from the Drishane knitting factory, went also to help to set it up.[47] It continued to give employment to the women in the area for almost thirty years, and the Sisters involved in it were also very close to the people. Sr St Mary Philomena went on business trips around the country several times a year and came back with valuable orders for the factory. The factory was very busy, especially in the months of November and December when the young women worked very hard, and very late with Sr St Mary Philomena and Sr Finbar, getting

---

[46] IJAD, Dr P Browne to Mother St Etienne Flahault, 20th March 1931.
[47] IJAD, *Ballyferriter Annals.*

Below: On the beach in Kerry

Above: Tig Ioseph, Ballyferriter
Below: On the beach in Kerry

out the orders that kept on pouring in. They were glad when the holidays came, because then there were always Sisters visiting from Drishane. Later on, when missionaries came on holidays, they also visited Ballyferriter from Malaya, Singapore and Japan as did Sisters from other congregations who stayed a few weeks in order to study Irish.

THE WAR YEARS

Meanwhile, the Boarding School and the School of Housecraft in Drishane both continued to provide a rich stream of recruits for the Novitiate. As soon as possible after profession, they were sent out to the missions in the Far East. The Second World War put a temporary stop to that. However, they could not all be kept in Drishane as there was not enough work for them in the schools and, in the Novitiate, new recruits were entering hot on their heels. Two Sisters, Sr St Columba (Sheila O'Donoghue, Glandore, County Cork) and Sr St Dolores (Mary Healy, Tralee, County Kerry) graduated from University in 1939 and, in September, were sent to Ballyferriter with twelve younger Sisters. Sr St Martin now had the extra task of feeding and housing fourteen young Sisters, but she and the other Sisters 'took it in their stride and were wonderful'. They had great memories of those days, of the pony, Sylvia, and of their occasional picnics earned by spring-cleaning the house.[48]

Mass started late on weekdays, giving time for 'a half an hour's meditation, a visit to the Blessed Sacrament, the Way of the Cross and our spiritual reading':

> Sunday was different. Mass was on time that day. We used to take little camp stools with us, and sit in the side aisle. The reason for this was that the local people had their own special pews, for which they apparently paid so we could not sit in them on a Sunday! ... The sermon used to go on and on, and there were only two topics, the same every Sunday, *An Cogadh, agus na daoine nar díol as na stolaca fós.*[49]

One of the Sisters in Ballyferriter throughout the War was Sr St Ernest (Julie Long, Kilcorney, Millstreet, Co. Cork). She had been in Penang for eight years and was to return there after the War for a further twenty years. Interestingly, she had worked as a stenographer in Duhallow Knitwear before entering the convent, cycling to Kanturk every day from her home in Kilcorney, so she had prior experience of the knitting industry.

SEPARATE COMMUNITY

In 1951 Ballyferriter was set up as a separate community from Drishane with Sr St Etienne (Stephanie Hyland, Monasterevan, Co. Kildare) as its first Superior. During this time a feature of the bungalow was that a small number of children came to board. They attended the local national school and learned Irish. In 1952, Margaret and Anne Kelleher and George and Rosemary Gleeson are mentioned in the Annals; Mary Fahy in 1953 and 1954; in 1960, Pauline Browne and Joy O'Connor were confirmed in Ballyferriter; in the same year, Pauline Browne and Ruth Carty joined their sisters in Drishane at the end of term and went home with them.

---

[48] IJAD, Sr Eilís Casey (formerly Sr St Xavier), *A Missionary Remembers.*
[49] Ibid. The War and the people who had not yet paid for their pews.

In 1957 the Sisters got their first cow.

> She was milked that evening by Madame St Martin and gave more than two gallons.[50]

Two years later they had their first threshing in one of the fields near the graveyard. Madame St Martin was delighted with the yield:

> 30 bags, the talk of the parish. It was a red letter day in the history of Tigh Ioseph.[51]

In 1962, Mother General was busy preparing for the General Chapter, so the canonical visit was made by Mother St Jeanne d'Arc and Mother St Anthony, Councillors. They were shown the farm, including the poultry. Mother St Jeanne d'Arc had never before seen battery hens and was greatly interested. However, she thought it was cruel that the poor hens could not run about freely.

In 1963, there was great excitement caused by the arrival of two sheep and two lambs which Reverend Mother St Benignus (Eilish Ahern, Ballyhooly, Co. Cork) had bought from the butcher in Dingle. Her idea was that they would eat the grass which was growing high around the house. Because four 'young professed' were visiting at the time - including Sr Peter their past pupil Mary Fahy – Reverend Mother christened the animals Paula, Peter, Helen and Eugene.[52] To the Sisters' dismay, Paula and Peter made their escape and sought their freedom on the mountain. When the Sisters returned from a walk up the mountain where they had hoped to find Paula and Peter, there was consternation once again: no trace of Helen and Eugene in the garden! They later found them, but failed in their efforts to entice them home.

MEMORIES OF BALLYFERRITER

Sr St Fergus (Deirdre O'Loan, Kanturk, Co. Cork) spent five months in Ballyferriter in 1953. She has particularly warm memories of 'Mollie', whose official name was Sr Finbar, a name which she and others seldom used:

> Mollie's melodious voice rings out as clearly in my memory today as it did fifty years ago... Her natural kindness came across in her beautiful brown eyes which so often gleamed with humour and a keen understanding of human frailty. Never for an instant was my lack of familiarity with the intricacies of making cardigans and pullovers held against me. Consequently I learned fast. Orders had to be met and great big boxes of finished garments had to be packed and dispatched by mail. The skills in packing I learned during that period remain with me today.
>
> My memories of the factory floor are bound up with the rhythmic sound of moving shuttles, the strange aroma of dampness which pervaded the work rooms as frequent showers drenched the heather-clad hillside against which the workrooms were built. But over and above all this was the lilt of melodious Irish voices, as all transactions among the workers were expressed in fluent Gaelic. Mollie's gifts of communication, however, transcended such requirements.

---

[50] IJAD, *Ballyferriter Annals*, 1957.
[51] IJAD, *Ballyferriter Annals*, 1959.
[52] Named after Sr Paula (Alice KilBride, Kanturk, Co. Cork), Sr Peter (Mary Fahy, Ovens, Co. Cork), Sr Helen (Wynne, Fermoy, Co. Cork) and Sr Eugene (Kate O'Neill, Baker Street, London).

Sr Finbar (Mollie) Murphy

Bean Ui Mhóráin stands out in my memory.[53] Her skill, her patience, her gracious acceptance of a "greenhorn" won my admiration. Her inner beauty shone in her careworn, lovely face and her use of Irish captured all the beauty and cadence of the language when used at its finest. My own love of Irish grew in this accepting community.

Somewhere in early or mid-September the call to return arrived, as registration for UCC loomed. Mollie was hilarious as she oversaw my exit. Months of fine wool particles had gathered between the pleats of the basque of my black dress. She did not think such evidence of industry was what I needed as I set out on a course of study, so she undertook a vigorous brushing of the offending bits of coloured wool.[54]

SYLVIA

Accounts of holidays in Ballyferriter often included reference to a trip in the pony and trap. The pony was called Sylvia and was Sr St Martin's pride and joy. Unfortunately, the day arrived when she had to be 'retired' to Drishane and the sadness of the community is reflected in the Annals:

> We were all very sorry, but Sr St Martin more than anybody else, to see our dear pony, Sylvia, being taken up to Drishane and leaving us for good. She had rendered great service to the community for about 22 years, drawing loads of many things necessary for the farm, drawing in the potatoes, hay etc. The holiday-makers enjoyed many a drive with her in the trap. It is a consolation for Sr St Martin in her grief at parting with her cherished pony, to know that the latter will be well cared for in Drishane. It was Sr St Paul's brother-in-law who took Sylvia up to Drishane in a special horse box attached to the back of his motor car. Reverend Mother and Sr St Paul (O'Flynn, Newmarket, Co Cork) left us the same day, accompanying Sylvia to her journey's end.[55]

Four of the 'knitting girls' got married within the year 1963-4, Peg Sears, Noreen Hoare, Eileen Long and Mary Ellen Manning, so the numbers in the factory were decreasing rapidly, with scarcely any newcomers. The reason given is that the girls now stayed on longer in education, many of them going in to Dingle to the vocational school. On the 29th July 1964 Reverend Mother announced to the 'knitting girls' that the factory was to be closed for good after the holidays. The house was to revert to its original use as a holiday home.

---

[53] A native of Ballyferriter, Bean Uí Mhóráin (Manning) returned there with her four children when her husband died in America.
[54] IJAD, Sr Deirdre (Fergus) O'Loan, Memories of Ballyferriter 1953 (typescript).
[55] IJAD, *Ballyferriter Annals*, 26th October 1960.

THE FOUNDATION OF MALAHIDE

PLANNING

CONSIDERATION OF VARIOUS POTENTIAL PROPERTIES

At the time of the purchase of Drishane in 1909, the Sisters were also pursuing the possibility of another foundation, Chaffpool House near Ballaghderreen in County Roscommon. But they really had their hands full with the establishment of the Novitiate, as well as the farm and the industries in Drishane, so the purchase of that particular second house was allowed to lapse. However, they always had it in their minds to have another base in Ireland.

Finnstown House, Lucan, County Dublin

In the 1940s the issue arose again. It started with a contact being made by a Mrs Massey of Perth House, Enfield with Arthur Cox, Solicitor, Dublin. She expressed an interest in acquiring Finnstown House at Adamstown, Lucan, County Dublin. Arthur Cox passed on her enquiry to the owner, Mr Cornelius Crowley of Millstreet. Mr Crowley's daughter, Mary (Sr St Cornelius), had entered the Novitiate in Drishane in 1935; Ann (Sr St Ann) in 1945; and a third daughter, Eta (Sr St Joan), was to enter in 1951. He instructed his solicitor to inform Mrs Massey that he was not free to negotiate with her at the time. He had other ideas for his property; he felt it might be an appropriate place for the Drishane Sisters to start a second school. Arthur Cox's reply to Mr Crowley stated:

> If I should happen to have the good fortune to meet His Grace I shall mention the Nuns to him but no opportunity for this has arisen since I last saw you and as you know I would not think that it would be good policy for me to write to him.[56]

Over the next fortnight, Arthur Cox made contact with a Monsignor Boylan and discovered that he knew all about it already, as it had come before the Diocesan Council:

> He told me that the difficulty is that once the House is established in the diocese the diocese has to look after it. There are already in Dublin Diocese more religious Houses than in the rest of the country. This imposes a heavy strain on the clergy, as it means that they have to provide a Priest, and so on. For these, and other reasons, they are not anxious to encourage new Houses, unless for absolute necessity.[57]

This is all very reminiscent of the correspondence with the Bishop of Kerry prior to the foundation of Drishane, including the major inconvenience for the diocese of having to provide a chaplain. On this occasion, though, Arthur Cox added that the Bishop of Kerry had already put in a good word. It is remarkable that almost forty years after the foundation of Drishane, the same two women - Mother St Beatrice now Superior in Drishane and Mother St Claire based in Paris for almost twenty years but still committed to the Irish project – are as innovative and as energetic in the pursuit of a second location for a school as they were at the start of the century in establishing Drishane.

---

[56] IJAD, Arthur Cox to C D Crowley, 4th July 1944.
[57] IJAD, Arthur Cox to C D Crowley, 17th October 1944.

Croom, County Limerick v Lucan, County Dublin

In 1946 another county[58] was being considered but Mother St Beatrice still seemed to be keen on the 'Crowley property'. So Mother St Claire visited the property with Mother General and they wrote to Mother St Beatrice from Weybridge on their return journey to Paris, weighing up the advantages and disadvantages of the two properties.[59] They concluded that neither the Croom nor the Lucan property would suit their needs. Their plan at this time was to open another School of Housecraft which, judging from their accommodation requirements, would be boarding. They wanted it to be near Dublin or another large town and they had a preference for a house that would offer all the required accommodation so that they would not have to embark on an expensive building programme. This was expecting a lot from any existing property

But Mother St Beatrice dug in her heels and kept up the pressure for Paris' agreement to her plan to purchase the house in Lucan. Mother St Claire, while trying to let her down gently, was firm in her opposition to it, as was Mother General:

> I understand your disappointment... on the subject of the result of our visit to Mr Crowley's house. The welcome of the Archbishop is really a small miracle. I also think that if it was only the condition of the house, so long unoccupied, there would be no hesitation – but it's a long way from Dublin! The Archbishop warned us on various points: the distance, the location, our livelihood, the possible work etc... Mother General checked two fine rooms which could do as the classroom/sewing room and the dining room. Then two other rooms the chapel and the community room...Mother worked out that you could have 25 beds there ... What good is that to receive at least 30 young women and the community?[60]

Although Mother St Claire insisted that a second foundation in Ireland was still being considered, a second foundation in England was becoming more urgent. On the day after their arrival in Weybridge, Mother General received a request for a school. In a typical gesture, Mother St Claire was rushing to get a letter in the post to Mother St Beatrice and she could not remember the name of the place where the proposed school was to be, just that it was where two of the Sisters went from Weybridge to teach Catechism. It would appear, therefore, that she was referring to Woking, Surrey:

> There's only a boys' school and the Headmaster of that school wants to expand and is going to set up a little further away in a nicer building. We have been to see it, the area is very pleasing to Mother, but the house on offer has nothing to recommend it. We need something else. Let's hope that something worthwhile turns up. There are pretty houses – the one that the Headmaster of the boys' school is going to take would have suited our needs, opposite the Catholic church... I'm sorry for Mr Crowley who went to so much trouble ... but really that cannot be a consideration in business matters.[61]

And Mother General added a post-script:

> No, my dear daughter, it is not a calamity not to agree to buy Mr Crowley's house: it's better to be sure than sorry! ... The Archbishop will not find it strange at all that we are not pursuing the Lucan project: He was kind, it is true, but not encouraging at all.[62]

---

[58] Limerick.
[59] IJAD, Mother St Claire to Mother St Beatrice, 8th March 1946.
[60] IJAD, Mother St Claire to Mother St Beatrice, 16th March 1946.
[61] Ibid.
[62] Ibid.

The correspondence continued, with Mother St Beatrice apparently making an official submission for approval, but once again meeting with firm opposition from the Mother House:

> Mother General has not changed her views on the subject of a foundation in Ireland (less important than Drishane) and a foundation in England (less important than Weybridge)... The Limerick house would appear preferable ... Finally, dearest Mother, Mother General ... wishes for the moment to await the reply of the Bishop. If it is in the affirmative, we shall study the question then.[63]

Again Mother General added:

> Please believe that I have not changed my mind: I wish to have another house in Ireland and another in England; but the house and the location must be convenient, and the borrowing not too heavy![64]

Within a couple of weeks approaches were made to the Bishop with regard to a foundation in Croom which, unfortunately, were not successful:

> ... It is the opinion of the Bishop that he has as many foundations as the Diocese can afford and on those grounds he has already refused two other recent similar applications. His Lordship regrets to have to give this decision as he thinks very highly of the great work your Communities are doing in many parts of the world, and if it were possible I think you would probably get the preference.[65]

Ballinagarde House

Two months later a Mr John Bowen was offering for sale Ballinagarde House, the yard and about 20 Irish acres for £6,000. In this case, the offer was forwarded to Mother St. Beatrice by 'KC', Howardstown.[66] KC's letter suggested that the House would be very suitable for a Convent, being on low ground but free from dampness, even though it had been unoccupied. The writer expressed caution, however, that if the Sisters were to view the property, the word would get out. This would suggest that the identity of the prospective buyers was being kept secret, probably because the Sisters could not buy a property without permission from the Bishop to establish themselves in his diocese – permission which was proving very hard to get – yet, at the same time, they had to have a property in mind in order to approach the Bishop with a proposition. Indeed, KC's letter went on to suggest that if permission could be obtained from the Bishop and Canons it would be a useful calling card if a suitable place turned up in some other diocese. The writer added, 'I'll do my own canvassing re Canons. I know well they like to be asked and canvassed too.' KC favoured Croom House, 'the one spot we would all think most suitable.'

[63] IJAD, Mother St Claire to Mother St Beatrice, 20th March 1946.
[64] Ibid.
[65] IJAD, W Hamilton PP Newmarket-on-Fergus to Mother St Beatrice, 2nd April 1946.
[66] IJAD, KC [Howardstown] to Mother St Beatrice, 12th [June] 1946. [Sr Ita Carroll's address is Howardstown, Bruree, Co. Limerick. Parents John and Catherine (K?)].

Bansha Castle

The correspondence picked up again the following year. This time the area in question was Tipperary and the correspondence was with Sr St Enda (Mary Angela Fitzgerald, Galbally, Co. Tipperary):

> A couple of days after your last visit to Bansha, I met Father Hayes and told him you and the Rev. Mother had interviewed the Bishop who had received you cordially and promised to submit your proposal for the establishment of a new Convent for the consideration of the next Diocesan Chapter... I will be willing to pay the cost of the car which brings you from Millstreet to Tipperary...
>
> PS I understand the views of Archdeacon Cooke carry great weight in Diocesan Councils. In fact any proposal strongly supported by him is not likely to be rejected. TPG[67]

It transpired that Mother St Beatrice had met Archdeacon Cooke many years earlier in the Duggan home in Douglas, Cork, so she wrote to him. (Her support for the Bansha property is confirmation that she has finally given in on the Crowley property in Lucan.) In reply, he informed her that

> The Archbishop summons the chapter for a meeting on Holy Thursday of each year, and probably your application will be discussed at our next meeting. Anything I can do to favour it will be gladly done.[68]

There is no record of the outcome of that diocesan chapter, nor, indeed of any visit by the Sisters to Bansha. However, Mr Givens and Fr Hayes were entertained in Drishane in May, and were totally captivated by its beauty:

> Father Hayes and I were delighted with our trip to Drishane and are very grateful to Rev. Mother, you and all the nuns for your hospitality. On our way back we said repeatedly we have had treatment today which could not be matched in the best of the luxury hotels. We also agreed that Drishane Convent must be one of the nicest if not the nicest in the country. Your magnificent buildings, their tasteful distribution in the beautiful grounds, and the grounds themselves with their trees, walks and avenues and waterways leave nothing to be desired. The placing of all these attractions in the forefront of the Muskerry Hills makes Drishane Convent a place, once seen, to be remembered all one's life.
>
> After this exhibition of the wonderful taste of your Community, I feel very flattered that you would have thought of making my place your second house in Ireland. This thought coupled with the covering of the trees in different tints of greenness make me appreciate this place in a way I never did before. I am enclosing a revised draft of the description of Bansha Castle and farms for your information. As I have no copy, I shall be thankful if you will please arrange to have it returned to me. I would have written sooner to thank Rev. Mother but I was waiting for the completion of this draft.[69]

This letter is ambiguous. On the one hand Mr Givens writes that he was flattered that the Sisters 'would have thought' of his home as a possible second home for themselves, which would seem to suggest that it was no longer a possibility. On the other hand, he encloses a revised draft of the description of Bansha Castle and farms, which would seem to suggest that it is still a live issue. In any event, the Sisters did not purchase in Tipperary.

---

[67] IJAD, Tom Givens, Bansha Castle, Tipperary to Sr St Enda (home on leave from Japan), 3rd March 1947.
[68] IJAD, N Cooke to Mother St Beatrice, 5th March 1947.
[69] IJAD, Tom Givens to Sr St Enda, 20th May 1947.

ESTABLISHMENT

INVITATION TO MALAHIDE

Mother St Beatrice completed her term of office as Superior in 1947; she died in 1948. It is a testament to her enormous energy and tenacity that, in the last years of her life, she was still battling with the authorities, ecclesial and congregational, to set up another base in Ireland. After Mother St Beatrice, the subject died down for a few years. But the meetings which the Sisters had had with the Archbishop of Dublin were not entirely in vain. Out of the blue in 1954 a letter arrived:

> Dear Reverend Mother,
>
> Some years ago you asked me for a foundation in this diocese in the Lucan district. It was not found advisable to grant your request at that moment. Now a suitable house and property is offered for purchase at Malahide, in my view, a much more advantageous proposal for your congregation. I would be willing to offer you a secondary school at this site.
>
> Such a foundation would be very useful for training your sisters for work in the missions, as you are close to the City. If you are prepared to consider my proposal, I should be grateful if you could call on Monday, 16th inst. at 12 noon. I would particularly request you not to divulge the project to any person, not even to your Sisters, except to your Council and only then in secrecy.
>
> I am, dear Reverend Mother,
> Yours sincerely in Christ
>
> +J C McQuaid
> Archbishop of Dublin[70]

It was to be four years (during which Abbeville, later the home of Charles J. Haughey TD, was one of the properties considered) before the purchase of the property in Bloomfield, Malahide was completed. In 1958, almost fifty years after the foundation of Drishane, the Sisters opened their second school in Ireland.

ARRIVAL OF FIRST SISTERS

On the feast of the Assumption, the 15th August 1958, Mother St Albert (Hannah McSweeney, Cork), Sr St Mary (Murphy-O'Connor, Cork) and Sr St Raphael (Catherine Moore, Castlemahon, Newcastlewest, Co Limerick) set out from Drishane by the 11 a.m. train 'full of the zeal and enthusiasm characteristic of Pioneers.'[71] The first days were marked by visits from Malahide families bringing gifts, arranging to drive the Sisters to Mass in the village, taking them out to see the neighbourhood and get their bearings. Most welcome of all were those coming to enrol their daughters in the new school. The first priest to visit was the Superior of the Columban Fathers, with a missionary who knew the Sisters in Japan and who brought a consecrated altar stone from one of their churches in the Far East, thus establishing the missionary link with the wider IJ family.

---

[70] IJAP, 6M 2-1 Drishane 1909-1967, 184. John C McQuaid, Archbishop of Dublin to Reverend Mother, Drishane Convent, 13th May 1954.
[71] IJAD, *Malahide Convent Annals Vol.I.*

*Above: Mrs Dowling with the pupils of her
school before the opening of Scoil Íosa.*

*Below: Scoil Íosa pupils in the 1960s with
L-R: Sr St Cyril Lovett; Mother St Albert
McSweeney; Sr St Alphonsus McMahon;
Sr St Mary Peter Weedle; Sr St Pius Lalor.*

Above: Sr Richard Nevill teaching in Scoil Íosa.

Below: Sr Gemma O'Dwyer with her cookery class.

Sr St Mary and Sr St Raphael returned to Drishane and were replaced by Sr St Fidelis (Mary O'Connell, Tralee, Co. Kerry) who was coming to stay in Malahide while she continued her studies in UCD, and Sr St Luke (Catherine O'Sullivan, Kilcummin, Co Cork). Sr St Alphonsus (Mary McMahon, Ballyheigue, Co Kerry) was to be the Head Mistress. They were soon joined by Sr St Fergus and Sr St Agnes (Ellen O'Connor, Abbeyfeale, Co Limerick). Work on the house was still going on when, after a blessing on Monday September 15th, the school opened its doors on Tuesday 16th to eighteen pupils. Mrs Dowling, who had her own small school in the village, joined the staff and brought her pupils with her. The first day is described in the Annals:

> All went off very well – only two catastrophes. A man fell through the ceiling while Sr St Fergus was teaching Latin. In this crisis the children were surprisingly quiet. While the ceiling was falling they seemed to understand that it could not be helped. This gave their mistress a high opinion of them. Sr St Alphonsus accidentally shut her classroom door on the inside. She forgot that the latch on the inside was broken off. She was locked into the room with the children. However, she brightened their spirits by asking them to sing. They got out of the room by one child going through the window and unlocking the door from the outside.[72]

Work on the house continued, in order to make it habitable for the Sisters and also suitable for the running of a school. The community grew in line with the needs of the growing school. In the early days, the Annals record the Sisters' joy at the enrolment of each new pupil. More Sisters joined the community – Sr St Richard (Eleanor Nevill, Ballybunion, Co Kerry), Sr St Cyril (Cláirín Lovett, Cork) took the girls for singing and Sr St Bríd (Mary de Courcy MacDonnell, Athy, Co. Kildare) for Art. Within ten years of its founding, there was a waiting list. The accommodation in the original house was supplemented with pre-fabs and a purpose-built assembly hall.

Because there was both a Junior School and a Secondary School, and that the Community house was also used as a base for Sisters from other communities when they were studying in the universities and colleges in Dublin, the number of Sisters who spent time in Malahide is very high. Among the teachers in the Junior School, in addition to those already mentioned, past pupils remember with great affection Sr Christine (Betty Kelleher, Widnes, Cheshire) who taught the Infant classes in the 1960s and again in the 1970s; Sr Margaret (Tarrant, Killarney, Co. Kerry) and Sr Marie Assumpta (Carmel O'Sullivan, Newcastlewest, Co. Limerick) who taught in the Junior School from the 1960s until the school closed; Sr Florence (Julia O'Sullivan, Rathmore, Co. Kerry) who was in charge of the Junior School for the final years of its existence.

NATIONAL DEVELOPMENTS IN EDUCATION POLICY

At this time, Government policy was having a major impact on the provision and management of second-level education in Ireland. In 1967 the Minister for Education announced the introduction of free secondary education (vocational education was already free). The Sisters had to make a decision: to continue to offer fee-paying education outside

[72] Ibid.

this free scheme, as some religious orders had decided to do, or to join the scheme and abolish the collection of tuition fees. The decision was taken in favour of the latter option for both the day school in Malahide and the boarding school in Drishane, as this was considered to be closer to the spirit of the Founder, Père Nicolas Barré.

Sr Raphael took over from Sr Alphonsus as Principal of the Secondary School in 1964. In 1972 the newly-built secondary school was officially opened by Dr John Charles McQuaid, Archbishop of Dublin. Sr Kathleen (Day, Whitegate, Co Cork) succeeded Sr Raphael in September of that year.

Meanwhile, a second Government decision was to have an even greater impact on the school in Malahide. The Minister for Education announced the introduction of a new type of school: the community school. The idea was that the pooling of resources on a larger campus would allow for greater subject provision and more efficient use of personnel. In some instances these schools were built from scratch where no school had previously existed; in others, the separate secondary schools for boys and girls amalgamated with the vocational school. The Department of Education planned one of these new schools for Malahide.

> There was huge opposition from the parents in Malahide – the girls' parents – they wanted this girls' school up on the hill for their girls. My own reaction was positive because I'd been in all co-ed schools before, I found it normal and natural, and the boys bring a certain kind of life. I was personally very pleased. And one of the reasons I was pleased was this could be handed over to lay people and I could return to mission life![73]

However, under pressure from parents to provide a sense of continuity, Sr Kathleen applied for the post and was appointed Principal of the new co-educational community school (Pobalscoil Íosa) in September 1976. The existing 1972 building continued to be used and was greatly augmented by a new school and sports hall on the same campus. Sr Kathleen retained the position of Principal for five years. She resigned her post in 1981, having seen one cohort through the second-level cycle. Then she started a whole new career as a pioneer missionary in Nigeria. The last Sister remaining on the staff, Sr Joan (Scannell, Rathcormac, Co. Cork) retired in 1985, bringing to an end almost three decades of IJ involvement in education in Malahide.

---

[73] Sr Kathleen Day, interview with the authors, December 2008.

WEYBRIDGE

The convents in England at Weybridge and Wolverhampton pre-date Drishane, and from the earliest days in Drishane there was movement between the two countries. Indeed, Weybridge and Wolverhampton provided the founding Sisters of Drishane. Mother St Claire Bringeon was Superior in Weybridge when she was appointed first Superior of Drishane; Mother St Anthony and Sr Joseph also came from Weybridge in 1909 and Sr Agnes (Margaret O'Flaherty, Meath) from Wolverhampton; Mother St Beatrice returned to Weybridge between her term as the first Mistress of Novices and her term as Superior in Drishane.

From its establishment in 1909, the Novitiate in Drishane supplied Sisters to England. In response to a request from Paris in 1948 for statistics, Mother St Albert, who was Novice Mistress at the time, wrote that Drishane had sent thirty-seven teaching sisters, in as many years, to Weybridge.[74] Many Sisters went on to spend their entire lives in Weybridge at St Maur's, an independent school for girls, or at Rosslyn House, an international finishing school. It is not possible in a publication such as this to do justice to all those Sisters who served in England throughout the century. St George's College Junior School, which is now co-educational, occupies the campus formerly occupied by St Maur's. St George's College itself, with which Sr Marie (Conheady, Newmarket-on-Fergus, Co. Clare) as Headmistress of St Maur's initiated a joint Sixth Form, now has a fully-integrated co-educational school on its own campus.

The only Sister still in Weybridge is Sr Mary (Murphy, Grimsby, England). Apart from ten years in Liverpool, Sr Mary has spent her entire IJ life in Weybridge since she was professed in 1951. Indeed she and her sister, Nora, were also at school in St Maur's. She provides, through her continuing presence, a valuable link between the Sisters and the past pupils and their families. Sr Mary has many friends in the area who greatly appreciate her continued presence there.

---

74 IJAP, 6M 2-1 Drishane 1909-1967, Mother St Albert to Mother House, 9th November 1948.

...de Famille	Prénoms	Pays	Départe...
Rodon	Marie	Loulans	Saône
Maclot	Marie Justine	Juriandville	Vos...
Déjean	Emma	Marseillan	Hé...
Cesterinde	Me Constance	Langres	H.te M...
Claerebout	Sclavia Hélène	Métèren	Nord
Lanon	P.te Claire Julia	Toulouse	H.te ...
Batts	Marie		Angl...
Canolly	Jeanne	Krabanne	Irland...
Desière	Marie, Antoinette	Métèren	Nord
Gabel	Hortense, Madeleine	Toulon	Var

PART TWO

Voyaging

de Religion.	N. de Famille.	Prénoms.	Pays.
décédée en Mai 8bre 1852. Paulin	Rodon .	Marie .	Loubans
intérieure 28 8bre 1852. Mathilde .	Naclor .	Marie Justine .	Surianville
intérieure 1 Février 1854. Damien .	Déjean .	Emma .	Marseillan
intérieure 22 Août 1863. Apollinaire .	Testevinde .	M. Constance .	Langres .
...draie .	Claerebout .	Sélanie Zélina .	Météren .
Euthyme .	Panon .	Frth. Claire Julie .	Toulouse .
F. Pulchérie	Batts .	Marie .	.
...grégoire .	Canolly .	Jeanne .	Strabanne .
...trick .	Devrière .	Marie, Antoinette .	Météren .
...éonard .	Gerbal .	Hortense, Madeleine .	Toulon .
...acharie .	Walterworth .	Marie, Sophie .	Londres .
Denis .	Walterworth .	Jenny .	Cherbourg
Théophile .	Pelletier .	Honorine, Marie .	Gevresin .
Albine .	de la Tablière .	Marie Hélène .	Aix .
...ean-Baptiste .	Kelly .	Hélène .	Kingstown.
Jeanne .	Fabrègue .	Caroline, Fanny .	Condras

*Above Front L-R: Sr St Martha Markey;
Mere Ste Mathilde; Sr St Francis de Sales
First Holy Communion. Yokohama 1887*

Penang Handwork Class with
Sr St Andrew Fitzgerald

CONTENTS

9 Cham... ...
...
10 Petite Salle
11 Petit avertir
12 Dégagement qui conduit...
13 Grande avertir
14 Cuisine
15 Dépense
16 Plonge...
17 Rigard ou endroit ...
   Voiture attendent ...
18 Jardin à ...
19 Chapelle 20 Jardin...

   Maison du centre
   qui sert en partie aux ...
1 Salle de récréation
2 dit comme aux Année
3 Réfectoire des orphelins
4 Dégagement
5 Imprimerie
6 Chambre où l'on relie
7 Parloir
8 petit parterre
9 Entrée principal de
10 Entrée qui conduit ...
11 Grand puits appart...
   autre fois à la ville
   Dans le haut est situ...
   shop tenu par les orp...
   la salle de commun...
   plusieurs chambre p...
   Sœurs 2 grand cham...
   servent de dortoir...
   infirmerie et 2 ...
   devent et derrière...

No.   Orphelinat
1 Bains
2 Lavoir
3 Cuisine
4 Dépense
5 Bains ou petit q...
   plus petites
6 Dégagement
7 ...ellier des grand...
8 Salle d'ouvrage
9 Salle d'armoires
10 ...cavier qui con...
   dortoir chambre

DRISHANE AND THE MISSIONS

THE VOYAGE OUT BEGINS

The mid-nineteenth century saw the expansion of the Institute outside France. During the reign of Louis XIV of France there was a request for Sisters to go to Siam (Thailand) but the King did not consider that such a journey was appropriate for young women. So, it was not until 1852 that the first group of Infant Jesus Sisters left from France to develop a mission in Malaya.

The group was sent out by the Mother General of the Institute, Reverend Mother de Faudoas, in response to an appeal from a Missions Etrangères de Paris priest, Père Jean-Marie Beurel, who was setting up Christian boys' schools. As early as 1851, Père Beurel was turning to the Institute seeking their help; recognising the need for schools for girls in Penang, he wrote to Mother de Faudoas. Five women were selected to go to Penang to establish a convent and school: Mother St Pauline Rodot, Sr St Pulcheria (Mary Harris, Bath), Sr St Eudoxie Claerbourt, Sr St Euthyme Panot and Sr St Rosalie Flammarion. They left France for Penang in December 1851, sailing from Antwerp, on board *La Julie*, on a journey which took over four months. The severity of the sea voyage and the tropical conditions into which they arrived took their toll on the Sisters. Mother St Pauline died during the voyage, and was buried at sea near Christmas Island, and only two of the remaining Sisters survived in sufficiently good health to begin developing a mission school.

The Apostolic Vicar to Malaya, Mgr Bouchot, sent an appeal for additional support and a second group of Sisters set sail for Penang late in 1852, arriving to help run the first Infant Jesus convent in Malaya. Among the group, who had made a difficult sea journey from Southampton on the maiden voyage of the *SS Benedick*, and then travelled overland by camel, was an Irish woman, Sr St Gregory (Jane Connolly, Strabane, Co. Tyrone). Sr St Mathilde Raclot and Sr St Damien Dejean completed the group. Sr St Gregory wrote back to her mother, who was living in France, assuring her that she was well and happy to be obeying the 'voice of God'. On finally arriving at Penang in late October, the Sisters were met by Sr St Eudoxie and Sr St Euthyme. Sr St Mathilde became the first Mother Superior (1852-54) in Penang. Writing home to the Mother House in Paris, she advised Mother General that the convent was a small house situated in the middle of a grove of cacao trees, near enough to the sea that the Sisters could benefit from a gentle breeze.

In 1859, the Sisters bought Government House, on Light Street, and the convent moved.[1] There they developed a novitiate and the first school for girls in Malaya. The premises became known as the Convent Light Street. Pupils came from wealthy Penang and Thai families, including children from the royal households of both countries. There were also 'second boarders' (pupils whose families could afford some fees), and orphans. The orphans were separated into different ethnic groups, and were allowed to speak in their native tongue until they were old enough to learn Malay and English. Some of the orphans attended school, while most helped the Sisters with domestic work and gardening.[2] There

---

[1] Light Street was named after Capt. Francis Light, the founder of the former British colony of Penang.
[2] Dilys Yap, *The Convent Light Street* (Malaysia: 2001), 14-15.

were several Irish Infant Jesus Sisters at the Penang convent in the nineteenth century: Sr St John Baptist (Helen Kelly, Kingstown [Dunlaoghaire], Dublin), who had been a postulant in Paris, went to Penang in 1861; Sr St Augustine (Margaret Coffey, Limerick) went there in 1885; and Sr St Veronica (Kitty Parker, Limerick) went in 1888. In 1893, Sr St Norbert (Honorine Hare, Cork) went out firstly to help care for the sick at Penang General Hospital, and in 1900 she moved to the convent at Bangkok. Sr St Bernard (Margaret Clifford, Cork) went out to Penang in 1899, and Sr St John (Anne Marie Brennan, Dublin) went in 1900.

There were also Irish Sisters at the convent in Singapore, which had been established by Mother St Mathilde and Sr St Apollinaire Testodive, Sr St Gregory Connolly and Sr St Gaétan Gervais in 1854, at Victoria Street. It had both a home for abandoned children and a school for girls, and was known as Town Convent. The 'baby gate' (later named the Gate of Hope) was the entrance at which orphaned and abandoned baby girls were left. The school also took fee-paying boarders. The end of the nineteenth century saw two additional Infant Jesus convents in Malaya: one in Taiping and one in Kuala Lumpur. In 1904, a convent opened in Seremban, and in 1907 the Sisters opened a new convent in Ipoh. These convents would become the destination for the first generation of Drishane Sisters once the Novitiate was established there in 1909.

The Roll Call of Irish women who were Infant Jesus Sisters working at mission convents in Malaya, before Drishane opened, is significant. These women spoke English which was the medium of instruction, so their contribution was particularly useful. By the end of the nineteenth century, the Institute had grown in the East; there were sixty-four English-speaking Sisters in Malaya, forty-four of whom were Irish. Additional English-speaking Sisters were needed, and Mother St Gaétan Gervais, Superior in Singapore, decided that it would be prudent to establish a Community in England to supply Sisters to Malaya which was at that time a British colony. Mother St Gaétan travelled to England, accompanied by Sr St Augustine (Kate MacSwiney, Kilmurry, Cork), arriving in London on 9th June 1892. Mother St Gaétan was, at this time, in poor health, and she died on 22nd August. Her plan to develop a Community in England that would supply Sisters for Malaya was not as successful as she had hoped. A convent was established in Weybridge in 1898, but the need remained to provide more English-speaking Sisters for the missions.

THE VOYAGE OUT FOR THE FIRST DRISHANE SISTERS

Mother St Beatrice Foley, the first Mistress of Novices in Drishane, had spent many years in Singapore and without a doubt she must have communicated her great love of the missions to the school girls and novices. A steady stream of Irish women, who entered in Drishane, went out to the missions. Records suggest that the first of these was Sr St Charles Borromeo (Ellen Whelan, Kildimo, Co. Limerick), who entered in 1910 and left for Singapore in 1912. Sr St Brendan (Elizabeth Brosnan, Killarney, Co. Kerry) became a postulant in 1912 and left for Kuala Lumpur in 1915; Sr Helena (Catherine Coveney, Kinsale, Co. Cork) entered in 1910 and went to Ipoh in 1915; Sr St Thomas (Hannah Fitzgerald, Bandon, Co. Cork) entered in 1913 and went to Singapore in 1915; Sr Finbarr (Mary Kennefick, Castlemartyr, Co. Cork) joined in 1912 and left for Kuala Lumpur in 1915; and Sr St Angela (Nora Fitzgerald,

Above: Ipoh Convent.
Below: Mère St Gaétan Gervais, Superior, Singapore 1883.

Galbally, Limerick) joined in 1913 and went to Seremban in 1916, though she later left the Institute in 1919. Thereafter, the Drishane Novitiate continued to supply large numbers of Sisters for the missions in Malaya and Japan. Their labour was particularly necessary with the opening of 'branch schools' in many rural areas near the main convents in Penang, Singapore, Kuala Lumpur and Ipoh, throughout the 1920s and 1930s.

DRISHANE SISTERS IN MALAYA

There is no doubt that the early generations of Drishane missionaries must have found their new circumstances quite extraordinary. However well prepared they had been by Mother St Beatrice, and despite receiving regular letters from the missions, the Sisters had to adapt to great change. They had to get used to the intense heat, different foods, new languages, and cultural differences that were a part of living in Malaya. What becomes clear from the Mission Annals and letters home from the Sisters is that they were united by their great sense of vocation and they were particularly energised by a desire to meet some of the needs of the poor who turned to them. What becomes equally clear, from published reflections by past pupils, is that the Sisters made a great difference to the lives of many children.

The growth of the Institute in Malaya was steady. In Penang, the Convent Light Street, and the orphanage buildings were extended significantly. By the time Drishane was sending out groups of missionaries, Light Street had built a new 'baby house', a library, dormitories and classrooms. The 1930s and 1940s saw the building of a beautiful chapel, and music rooms. Pupils from the school attained distinction in both Government examinations and Junior Cambridge examinations, firmly establishing the Infant Jesus convent at the centre of education for girls in Penang. In 1927, the convent bought a dilapidated house on the beach at Tanjong Bungah, which became a welcome holiday home for the Sisters and the orphan children. In 1934, the Institute built a convent at Balik Pulau, and that same year they also opened a convent in the Cameron Highlands.

Drishane Sisters made an important contribution teaching the children and supplying stability and comfort. Past pupils who were at the orphanage, day school and boarding school in Penang during the 1930s and 1940s have left accounts of how they experienced security and routine, through regular mealtimes, prayers, and lessons. Lorna Aeria (née Rodrigues) was one of a family of eleven children, whose mother died in 1934. Four of the children were sent to the convent, and Lorna – who was just one year old – was placed in the 'baby house'. Later, when she joined her sisters in the boarding school, she was taught by Irish Sisters including Sr St Columba (Mary Kate Madden, Roscrea, Co. Tipperary) and Sr St Dunstan (Lizzie Keegan, Rathaspick, Co. Laois). Lorna recalled Sr St Columba as having 'great gentleness and a great sense of humour, but at the same time she was strict.'[3] The children were well-fed, and Lorna recalled that Sunday breakfast might include sausage, while lunch was rabbit or meat curry with potatoes. The children rose early to pray at 5.30 am. Breakfast was typically bread and butter, with cheese, jam or bananas, and a cup of tea. Lessons took place from 8 am until noon, at which time the children lunched on rice,

3 Ibid., 64.

meat or fish, and vegetables. School continued in the afternoon, and tea and a biscuit was provided to the children at 4.30, before playtime. The boarders studied from 6 pm to 7 pm, and dinner was then served. Prayers and bed followed. There were occasional treats, which all children appreciated. When the breadfruit tree came into season, the children were given some with brown sugar, and they also enjoyed banana cake.

The Sisters gave the children a few cents once a month, to buy sweets or fried noodles in the tuck shop, and they also gave special food supplements to pupils who were delicate. For example, Lim Pee Chin, who was sent to the Penang convent in 1935, recalled that children who were weak, or recovering from an illness, were visited in class at 10.30 am by a Sister who would give them a cup of Horlicks and a beaten egg. She also recalled that all pupils were given cod liver oil every day. Pee Chin, who was one of seven children, did not see her family very often as they lived quite far from the convent. Life at the convent was particularly important to such pupils. Pee Chin recalled being brought on holidays with other pupils to the beach house at Tanjong Bunga, and going for school picnics on Penang Hill. Reverend Mother St Tarcisius became her Godmother. Later when Pee Chin had completed her studies she took typing and shorthand classes at the convent and during her Easter holidays she would stay back to work on these skills with Sr St Fabian (Anna Mary Butler, Ballyhennebry, Co. Kilkenny), an Irish Sister who was also fondly remembered by another pupil, Oh Eng Sim, for her excellent teaching of sports.

DRISHANE SISTERS IN SINGAPORE

Town Convent, Singapore, also made great strides in developing a reputation for excellence in teaching. By 1905, pupils sat both the Junior Cambridge and Senior Cambridge examinations. By the 1920s, the Sisters had introduced sports and there was also an orchestra. Each year, the pupils would hold a week-long exhibition, attended by 'high-ranking colonial officials and wealthy businessmen', at which the pupils 'displayed their art and needlework, and staged musical and dramatic performances.'[4] As the convent grew in reputation, the Sisters found they had to expand the premises. In 1931 they bought the Hotel Van Wikl, and started a Chinese school there, which eventually became St Nicholas's Girls School.

The Irish Infant Jesus Sisters who were at Singapore in the early decades of the twentieth century included Sr St Daniel Walsh, Sr Gertrude (Ellen Fehily, Enniskean, Co. Clare), Sr St Thomas Fitzgerald, Sr Agatha (Sarah Flynn, Glenfarne, Co. Leitrim), Sr St Benedict (Johanna O'Connell, Innishannon, Co. Cork), Sr St Mark (Kate Cuffe, Glanmire, Co. Cork), Sr St John (Josie Desmond, Mossgrove, Bandon, Co. Cork), Sr St Gerard (Magdalene McCourt, Bambridge, Co. Down), Sr St Anselm (Eily Galvin, Kenmare, Co. Kerry), Sr St Lawrence O'Toole (Mary Turner, Mallow, Co. Cork), and Sr St Elizabeth (Mary Teresa McSweeney, Farnanes, Co. Cork).

These Sisters arrived out to work at a school that was orderly and efficient. The day-to-day life at the schools in Singapore has been documented by one past-pupil, Elaine Meyers, in her book *Convent of the Holy Infant Jesus: 150 Years in Singapore*. They found themselves

---

4 Elaine Meyers, *Convent of the Holy Infant Jesus: 150 Years in Singapore* (Singapore: 2004), 53.

teaching in high-ceilinged classrooms that were laid out 'very formally... desks arranged in single file, each with a big ink pot and ink well... about 25 desks in each room.'[5] In the 1930s, the girls at Town Convent wore a simple dress, in 'convent blue', with a Peter Pan collar. The blazon was pinned to the collar, and the dress was belted. Even though the pupils followed an academic curriculum, they were also obliged to learn to sew, cook, iron and do laundry, as such domestic work was considered an important part of preparation for marriage and motherhood. At Town Convent, the girls also learned European cooking, and special utensils and ingredients were imported to facilitate this. They also developed a sense of *esprit de corps,* through learning to play team sports; the Sisters introduced the 'house' system – whereby pupils in the red, blue, yellow and green houses sported their coloured ribbon during netball matches, a system similar to the 'house' systems found in many Infant Jesus schools. Meyers also recalled:

> ... [that] religion pervaded the school's atmosphere...prayers were said daily; in the morning, before each lesson and in the afternoon. Catholic girls were taught catechism...during Lent the girls went on a two to three day retreat.

The girls were encouraged to demonstrate character-building, a practice which many past pupils recalled as having given them the strength to withstand hardship during the Japanese occupation. Another past-pupil, Elizabeth Choy, observed:

> I was very lucky to be able to get into the Convent of the Holy Infant Jesus... We had a very good grounding in be[ing] courageous, to trust in God... otherwise without all this background I'd never have been able to go through the Japanese period in the Occupation and the tortures.[6]

Elaine Meyers has also recalled the kind of 'pre-war discipline' that was part of the legacy of the Infant Jesus Sisters. She wrote:

> Exemplars of discipline were the nuns themselves. Their upright conduct was discipline itself, reinforced by their heart-stopping black robes and cowls. The nuns could always be seen working, teaching or praying in the chapel. Their physical presence, their gentle but firm leadership and their dedication to their mission created a religious atmosphere and imposed a sense of discipline. Shouting, hitting and other aggressive acts of control were not required by the nuns; one look from a cowl-framed face was more than sufficient to bring an errant student into line.[7]

There were many Drishane Sisters who made a huge contribution to this 'pre-war' legacy. These women were to be situated at the centre of the Pacific Theatre of War, when the Japanese invaded Malaya on the 8th December, 1941.

DRISHANE SISTERS IN JAPAN

As we have seen, the Institute had established itself in Penang in 1852 and Singapore in 1853. In 1872, Fr Petitjean, Apostolic Vicar to Japan, wrote to Mother St Mathilde in Singapore and asked for some Sisters to come to teach in Japan. He needed their support immediately, so a telegram was sent to France to ask Mother de Faudoas for her permission

---

[5] Ibid., 57-58.
[6] Ibid., 58.
[7] Ibid., 59.

*Above: Yokohama, 1889. Back L to R: Sr Louise, Sr St
Adeline, Sr Gertude. Front L to R: Sr St Francis de Sales, Sr
St Bernard Clifford, Sr St Martha Markey, M St Mathilde,
Sr St Xavier, Sr St Guillaume, Sr St Mary.*

*Below: Drishane in Singapore with, centre,
Mother St Claire Bringeon*

and her blessing for the departure of some Sisters. She sent her agreement by return. Sr St Norbert Levesque was named as the first Mother Superior of the new foundation in Yokohama, and it is reported that she responded to the news with both 'fear and joy' and became 'as pale as death and unable to speak'. Sr St Gregory Connolly and two French Sisters, Sr St Gelase and Sr St Ferdinand, were also chosen to go from Singapore to help found the new convent at Yokohama. Within ten days, the Sisters commenced their voyage from Singapore to Hong Kong, and then on to Yokohama where they landed on 28th June and established the first Japanese foundation.

The Yokohama convent had an orphanage and a workshop, but it became known for its school – St Maur's (later St Maur's International School) – which provided education for the international community irrespective of religious denomination. It also had a Japanese school, the Koran Gakko (later Futaba). In 1875, a second house was founded in Tokyo, with a school to educate Japanese primary and secondary pupils. A third foundation was opened in Shizuoka in 1903, to educate Japanese children from families who worked in agriculture and industry. Among those Irish Sisters whose mission was Yokohama at the end of the nineteenth century were Sr St Oswald (Bridget McDonald, Ennis, Co. Clare), and two sisters, Sr St Mary (Annie Keegan, Rathaspick, Co. Laois) and Sr St Dunstan (Lizzie Keegan).

The Communities in Japan suffered a number of hardships in the early decades of their ministry. In 1884 the buildings in Yokohama were devastated by a typhoon, and in 1894 an earthquake demolished the school. But the Sisters were not deterred, and they rebuilt their schools. To expand further, a Novitiate was opened in 1921 after which time the number of Japanese Sisters increased. At that stage, Sisters from the Novitiate in Drishane had also arrived to Japan. Sr St Teresa (Kate O'Donoghue, Lissarda, Co. Cork), was the first to go from Drishane to Japan in 1910. She returned to Drishane in 1922 due to ill health and lived there until 1981. Other Irish Sisters included Sr St Denis (Kathleen Twohig, Clontarf, Dublin), Sr St Agnes (May Hayes, Kilmallock, Co. Limerick), and Sr St Peter (Kate O'Mahony, Cork City). Disaster struck Yokohama again in 1923, when the Great Kanto Earthquake took place on 1st September, demolishing all of the Infant Jesus buildings completely. The Institute in Paris recorded that this earthquake had '... destroyed in thirty seconds, the result of fifty years toil.'[8] Sixteen pupils and ten Sisters were killed. Among them were Sr St Wilfrid (Bridget Sweeney, Co. Clare), and the two sisters from Co. Laois, Sr St Dunstan Keegan and Sr St Mary Keegan.

The Sisters who survived the earthquake worked for hours to rescue others from the debris, before the police finally removed them from the area and they were given temporary refuge on a steamer ship, *André Lebon,* until they could make their way to the convent in Tokyo. Exactly two months later, the Sisters had recommenced their mission in Yokohama. They went there daily from Tokyo to teach homeless orphans and pupils of the Koran Gakko, in a temporary shelter that had been set up in the ruins of the Marianist College.

---

[8] The Mother House Paris, *The Charitable Mistresses of the Holy Infant Jesus, known as the Dames de St Maur, 1662* (Paris: Published in the Mother-Generalship of Reverend Mother Ste. Marguerite-Marie Delbecq, 1924).

In the years that followed, Drishane sent out additional support to Japan. Sr St Marcienne (Sarah McGann, Ennis, Co. Clare) and Sr St Lelia (Vera Rutledge, Ballinamore, Co. Leitrim) arrived in Yokohama in 1924, followed a year later by Sr St Lucy (Brigid Burns, Cahirciveen, Co. Kerry). Sr St Rita (Eileen Keegan, Killarney, Co Kerry) went to Shizuoka in 1926, while her sister, Sr St Bernard (Mary Keegan) went to Yokohama in 1930. And another set of siblings from Ardfert, Co Kerry, also found their mission in Japan at this time: Sr St Winifred (Johanna Lyne), Sr St Veronica (Winifred Lyne), and Sr St Christopher (Eileen Lyne). These three Sisters would be interned together when the War in the Pacific broke out in 1941.

WORLD WAR II

The narrative of history tells us of how Japan pursued its military offensive in Malaya. It is a narrative that positions the Japanese and the Malayans as enemies at that time. Within that narrative there are many other complex histories, which do not find expression in accounts of the terror and violence of the War. One of those histories is that of the Infant Jesus Sisters: they had foundations in Malaya and Japan at the outbreak of the War and these women were Sisters in Christ. Their story is, therefore, one in which political and public enmities had no place, and their work transcended national differences. Their long history of mission in both Malaya and Japan served them particularly well at this challenging time.

The War in the Pacific broke out in December 1941, when the Japanese struck Pearl Harbour and incapacitated the US Pacific fleet. Immediately, Japan could pursue its military objectives in the Pacific, which included Malaya, from Penang to Singapore, all areas in which there were Irish Infant Jesus Sisters. The Japanese 25th Army advanced quickly into Malaya on 8th December, commencing the Battle of Malaya. Penang was bombed daily from the 8th to the 17th of December, at which time it was abandoned, and Europeans were evacuated. By the end of the first week of January 1942, the Japanese army had taken Northern Malaya, and it moved down into Kuala Lumpur where it took occupation on the 11th January, just 200 miles from Singapore island. The Allied forces were forced back to Johore, on the southern tip of Malaya, and they retreated into Singapore on January 31st. The Japanese completed their rapid advance through Malaya when they crossed to Singapore, landing some 30,000 Japanese troops and advancing through the island, cutting off food and water supplies, and forcing surrender. The fall of Malaya was witnessed by many Infant Jesus sisters who found themselves caught in the centre of an aggressive and unstoppable Japanese offensive, which overwhelmed British, Indian, Australian and Malayan forces who tried to defend the colony.

Nothing could have prepared the Irish Sisters for what they witnessed during the weeks of attack, and afterwards during occupation. Yet in one of the last letters that Sr St Francis Xavier (Annie O'Shea, Newmarket, Co. Cork) managed to send from Kuala Lumpur to Ireland after the outbreak of war, her thoughts were firmly with Drishane and the novices that she hoped she would soon welcome to the missions:

> The War may have succeeded in widening the material distance between us, but it is a
> consolation at the same time to think that no torpedo or submarine can interfere with our
> communications on high... How grand it will be all the same when peace is restored once
> more... what a joy it will be to see the boat arriving with the first batch of post-war Missionaries!
> It does not matter that the Sisters here will be so old that you will not recognise any of
> them as Drishane acquaintances... we are all one family and I can assure you, you will feel
> that before you feel the heat![9]

The War was to continue until 1945, cutting all communication between the mission
convents and Drishane. At an early stage, the Sisters at Penang, Ipoh and Taiping were all
obliged to evacuate. Penang convent was occupied by the Japanese and turned into a prison
for American Prisoners of War. The Sisters, orphans and babies from Ipoh were moved
south to Klang, and then to Kuala Lumpur convent where they found that the convent
at Cameron Highlands had also evacuated to Kuala Lumpur. The evacuation of the Ipoh
group to Klang is documented in a post-war letter written by Sr St Lawrence (Annie Mc
Cusker, Lurgan, Co. Down) to the community at Drishane:

> ...when the train came in... 120 came off all terrified in the dark. There was the lame and
> blind, each one had her fortune tied up in a yard and a half of new calico... You should
> have seen Reverend Mother Tarcisius when they arrived. Different shoes etc and clothed
> in night gowns, as it was a night flight for them.[10]

The evacuation of the Taiping community to Seremban is also recorded. During that night
the elderly Sr St Michael became very weak and had to be removed by stretcher from the
train, and Sr St Etienne sat with her while the station master called for an ambulance. At
that point, an air raid sounded, and everyone scrambled from the train and ran to a shelter
under ground. The Sisters, helped by a man from the train, brought the stretcher bearing
Sr St Michael into the shelter. Later that day, Sr St Michael died. The Sisters at Seremban
later clearly remembered 'the orphans of Taiping arriving at night in the dark, exhausted,
each carrying a bundle of her own and some provisions, and hanging from her neck, a
mug. It was a unique procession from the station to the convent, where they remained for
a few months.'

DRISHANE SISTERS IN MALAYA DURING THE WAR

At Teluk Anson, Mother St Odon (Bridget Dempsey, Kilkenny) managed to stay at the
convent despite having a struggle to make ends meet. The attacks on Teluk Anson
commenced on the 26th December 1941, just as the Sisters were making their Spiritual
Reading. They heard the drone of planes, and just managed to get into the air raid shelter
under the convent staircase when the bombing commenced. The convent was not hit, and
the Sisters were able to take in refugees who had been injured. For days afterwards, Japanese
soldiers came and went from the convent, and the Sisters were frightened. Finally, an Edict
was provided by a Japanese Commander, which was posted on the convent gate, forbidding
soldiers to enter the grounds. The Japanese authorities allowed the Sisters at Teluk Anson to
recommence their teaching, with the clear instruction that no English was to be taught. By
December 1942, the Japanese turned the convent into a Government school and appointed

---

9 IJAD, Malaya Notebook, *Malaysia-Singapore Annals.*
10 IJAP, Mission in Malaya (1852-1945). Typescript 5th August 2002.

a headmaster. Throughout the Occupation, the Sisters at Teluk Anson worked at sewing, and even shoemaking and doll-making, in order to make money; so successful were they at these enterprises that they eventually had to turn down orders for work.

In Singapore, the boarding school pupils were on their Christmas break when the first bombs fell. The orphans and Sisters took refuge in an air raid shelter which was erected near the convent, and some Carmelite nuns and pupils of the Good Shepherd Sisters also stayed there with them. Singapore convent was struck by seven bombs on the 14th February 1942, and heavy bombing continued through the next day, when Singapore capitulated. At the convent, the orphanage, chapel, main gate, and school field were all hit. Part of the house remained habitable, so some of the community, including Sr St John Desmond chose to remain at the convent.

Two months after the Japanese occupation of Singapore, the convent was re-opened under Japanese authority, and renamed Victoria Street Girls' School. English was removed from the syllabus; Japanese was introduced, and teachers and pupils were taught about Japanese culture. Life during the Occupation was harsh. Food was rationed, so the Sisters grew fruit and vegetables. Throughout the War, homeless and destitute people arrived at the convent looking for shelter, and the Sisters also took in many orphaned children. In August 1943, about forty Sisters together with orphans and some teachers from Town Convent, were among the thousands of people that the Japanese deported from Singapore to two voluntary internment camps in Malaya.[11] This group included Mother St Charles and Sr St Columba, who took the orphans with them from Singapore in the hope that they would all be safer there. They were brought by trucks and train to Bahau, in Negri Sembilan, where they had to live in huts in the middle of the jungle where there was no water supply. The Sisters dug wells, made utensils from branches and leaves, and grew root vegetables. Life was intensely difficult during the War, and while no Sisters died as a result of combat, they suffered from the kinds of diseases that flourished in the severe living conditions. For example, Sr St Raphael (Elizabeth O'Brien, Middleton, Co. Cork) and Sr St James (Mary Conheady, Newmarket-on-Fergus, Co. Clare) both died from dysentery.[12]

The Ipoh community, which had taken temporary refuge at Kuala Lumpur, was allowed to return to the convent at Ipoh in August, 1942. There they learned that the Japanese had occupied the convent and the Sisters were instructed to remove all of their religious pictures and crucifixes from the building, and that they 'could take up farming if they wished.' They quickly set about storing some of the convent furniture in the houses of their old neighbours. In September, they were told that they could stay at the orphanage, where they were interned until the end of the War. They were allowed out only to attend daily Mass and to go to the market. They were obliged to learn Nippon-go (Japanese language), and many of the Sisters found it very difficult to master. They also took in some pupils for lessons in shorthand, typewriting, French, Latin, and mathematics. This gave some income, and kept the Sisters very busy as their little school became very popular. The Sisters also took in needlework, as they had a good supply of thread at a time when little could be bought in the shops. They planted vegetables, on three acres of land, and Reverend Mother bought a cow so that milk could be provided for the babies. The sisters worked hard together, and somehow found joy during these years. Sr St Helen (Nora O'Sullivan, Killinardrish, Co.

---

[11] See Meyers, *150 Years in Singapore*, 61.
[12] IJAD, Sr St John Desmond to Mother St Beatrice, 6th September 1945.

Futaba, Japan, May 1945.

Cork) interned at the orphanage at Ipoh, recalled:

> Our bags were always packed ready to march off to the internment camp... [we had] whole nights of prayer, and we practised during these years the poverty of our early Sisters... we drank our black sugarless coffee with joy and gladness of heart. It was perhaps the happiest time of our lives – one and all will agree to that... we can always look back on it as a time of close Union with God and joy and peace of heart, and I am glad to add – intense union in our happy little home. [13]

DRISHANE SISTERS IN JAPAN DURING THE WAR

In Japan, at the outbreak of the War, the Irish Sisters were in an invidious position. Because they taught Japanese children and had Japanese Sisters within their communities, they had many friends who were Japanese. But the Irish Sisters were officially the enemy, because they were perceived as being British. Before the outbreak of the War, the Sisters had taken out passports at the British Embassy. Sr St Teresita, who spent most of her life in Japan, recalled this process:

> Shortly before World War II started, the Japanese Government decided that all foreigners should have a special residence permit for Japan that would be renewed every three years. In order to get such a permit, each foreigner had to present her/his up-to-date passport... [but the Infant Jesus Sisters] came to Japan with the understanding that it was for life and that there would be no home-leave! With that in mind, they packed their passports away ...until the notification...[by which time] they were all out of date! Frantically the Irish sisters went in haste to the police station to explain their dilemma. The authorities calmly suggested that they would go to the British Embassy and ask for new passports. So off they went and in no time were issued with beautiful new ones with which they procured their residence permits.[14]

Shortly after the outbreak of the War, the police came to the convent to take away the passports of foreign Sisters, including the British passports held by the Drishane Sisters. A day later, they returned to round up all the Sisters, giving them thirty minutes to pack their things before taking them to Denenchofu to be interned at one of their own convents and orphanages which had been turned into a camp. As was customary in such camps, a daily roll call, or 'tenko', was taken at which time internees were grouped with members of their own nationality. One Irish Sister, Sr St Francis Xavier MacSwiney, a sister of Terence MacSwiney, at first refused to comply with the demand to line out with British internees, answering firmly, 'I'm NOT British'. However, she was obliged to obey orders. The Irish Sisters remained interned at Denenchofu for two years; they were then moved to a Franciscan monastery at Sekiguchi for two months, at which time the police released them on the grounds that it had become clear that they were Irish, and not British.

Sr Clare (Ursula O'Callaghan, Mossgrove, Bandon, Co. Cork) has noted that once the War broke out, the Sisters quickly placed their Japanese Sisters in all of the positions of seniority in the convents, even if this meant having a relatively young and inexperienced Japanese Sister take over such a position. For example, Sr St Cecilia Takamine Nobuko was made Principal of Futaba at the age of twenty-eight.[15] But such precautions did not prevent the

---

[13] IJAD, Sr St Helen O'Sullivan to Sr St Mary Magdalen and Mother St Beatrice, September 1945.
[14] IJAD, Japan Collection.
[15] Sr Clare O'Callaghan, interview with the authors, 15th July 2008.

schools from being in the line of fire. Sr St Teresita (Ellen Dwyer, Drogheda, Co. Louth) recalled, with remarkable calm, the complete destruction of the Sisters' work in Japan: '...Yotsuya (novitiate), [and our] convents and schools in Yokohama, Shizuoka and Fukuoka were demolished, but no lives were lost. Thanks be to God.' The day after Futaba was destroyed, the Sisters returned to the site to take stock of the damage. All of their buildings, which had been made from wood, were burnt down; only the concrete chapel remained.

OTHER INTERNEES WRITE ABOUT THE DRISHANE SISTERS

Because communication with Europe was virtually cut off during the War, the Sisters could not write to Drishane or to their families. Records of their lives during this period are therefore scant. A few surviving letters from the mid-1940s that arrived safely in Drishane during and immediately after the War, contain second-hand accounts of the Sisters in Japan, written by people who had met them in internment camps and at the convents. These accounts tell us about the extraordinary impact that the Sisters had on those with whom they were forced to live, and those who needed their comfort and support. One such letter came from a Protestant woman who had been interned with sixteen Irish Infant Jesus Sisters in Tokyo between September 1942 and October 1943. Among this group were three siblings from Ardfert, Co Kerry: Sr St Winifred Lyne, Sr St Veronica Lyne, and Sr St Christopher Lyne.

> Motorship Gripsholm, Japan   November 1st 1943
>
> Dear Madame
>
> When I left Japan, I promised the mother and sisters of your order that I would write you to tell you of their welfare. There were fourteen Irish sisters in the camp... Sr St Virgilius (Mary Murray, Broadford, Co. Clare) took her vows at the beginning of the year and they were all happy for her...Sr St Lelia and Sr St Rita kept us all laughing. They each seemed to have some special gift and became to me very much like my own sisters. [The camp]...was one of your buildings, but so comfortable for your sisters to be in their own Convent even though they had to crowd into four of their rooms. The two older mothers were in a separate room and quite comfortable...They used one room as their kitchen and had four beds in the other part... They were such good cooks, Sr St Teresita and Sr St Veronica especially, and they made good little cakes, always sharing them.

The letter continued to praise the skills of Sr St Teresita, who could somehow 'camouflage' the taste of the food supplied by the camp cooks; she would take the food and 'cook it over', to make it palatable and to ensure that the internees would eat it. Simple supplies, such as macaroni soup and spinach, were made tasty with the addition of breadcrumbs. The prayers and comfort that the Sisters provided for other internees were also noted:

> ...their lives are being of use even though it cannot be the way they would choose... Their willingness to endure the trials of internment means much to their Japanese friends... You need have no concern. They are willing to face the worst that can come... I have written at length but feel that I have not done justice to your Irish sisters. I am a Protestant but was much impressed by the beauty of their lives and their utter devotion and felt I must express my gratitude to their home for sending forth such noble women. I trust that they may be soon given freedom or be repatriated – whatever is God's will for their lives.[16]

---

[16] IJAD, Katherine Greenbank to Reverend Mother St Beatrice, 1st November 1943. In this camp at Sumire Gakuin, Tokyo, were Mother St Enda, Sr St Peter, Sr St Francis Xavier, Sr St Teresita, Sr St Denis, Sr St Francis, Sr St Pascal, Sr St Winifred, Sr St Veronica, Sr St Christopher, Sr St Paul, Sr St Mary Veronica, Sr St Rita, and Sr St Lelia.

CHINA: THE MISSION AT MOUKDEN 1936-1946

Little detail is known of the ten years during which the Infant Jesus Sisters had a convent at Moukden, China. However, existing records clearly show that Sr St Aidan (Kitty Fitzgerald, Bandon, Co. Cork), the Irish Sister who was its first Superior, was remembered with great admiration by those who knew her in China. The Bishop of Moukden, Monseigneur Blois, asked the Infant Jesus Sisters to come to Moukden in 1936. Five Sisters, one each from Japan, Spain, Italy, Poland and France, were sent with Sr St Aidan to found the convent at Moukden. During the War, Sr St Aidan was noted for her charity to those who were interned at the Moukden Club, near the convent. Some accounts of her work reached Drishane in 1945 and 1946, in letters from people who had met her. In November 1945, Fr Kennedy SJ wrote to Drishane to advise that he had recently seen Sr St Aidan and had several talks with her. He was very aware of the dangers that she faced as she secretly provided help to internees:

> ...she was not interned. No one knows why. But those who were interned thanked God that she was left free. She managed to help them a lot by smuggling in forbidden things...While I was there she was up against a new problem: drunken Russian soldiers. However, before we left she had got a permanent guard from Russian H.Q. She was also housing and trying to look after refugees: Germans thrown out of their houses by the Russians, and Japanese women and children who came into the convent grounds for shelter at night-time. As far as I could see, the first place anyone in trouble went to was to your Sister. And they never went in vain.[17]

Sr St Aidan died only ten years after her mission to China had begun. Like some of the other Sisters with whom she worked in Moukden, she contracted typhus while working amongst infected refugees. The final illness and death of Sr St Aidan is recorded in a letter from Sr St Marie Bernadette to Revered Mother in Drishane, written on 7th March, 1946, in which she said 'Sr St Aidan visited the Japanese refugees, brought three Japanese orphans back to the convent, washed them herself [and became] infected with typhus.'[18] Between 14th and 17th March, six sisters at Moukden had contracted the disease, and the congregation had to turn to the Bishop to ask him to send them nurses to tend the dying Sisters. By 6th April, Sr St Marie Bernadette had herself succumbed to tuberculosis, and a letter addressed to Mother General advised that there was no hope of her recovery.

DRISHANE AND THE MISSIONS AFTER THE WAR

When the War ended on 15th August 1945, there was a period of transition, as the British troops moved in to take control from the Japanese. The Infant Jesus Sisters were keen to get back to work and there are some surviving accounts of their great industry at this time. Sr St Helen, writing to Drishane from Ipoh, described how the sisters took repossession of Ipoh convent and immediately set about 'scrubbing, washing and disinfecting'. By 26th September, their school at Ipoh was ready to reopen its doors, with 800 pupils registered. Within two months, that number had risen to 1600.[19]

The Sisters, unsurprisingly, wrote to Ireland to encourage Drishane to send more Sisters to

[17] IJAD, Fr R Kennedy SJ to Reverend Mother St Beatrice, 30th November 1945.
[18] IJAD, Sr St Marie Bernadette to Reverend Mother St Beatrice, 7th March, 1946.
[19] IJAD, Sr St John Berchmans to Sr St Francis of Assisi, 10th October 1945.

help with all the work that remained to be done. Sr St Helen encouraged Drishane to send support to Ipoh, while Sr St John Desmond wrote from Singapore, hoping that some new Sisters were coming out. She wrote to Mother St. Beatrice, saying '...I hope Mother Albert has a strong body of recruits to send us out soon. We are old, not so up to date, and if we want to hold our own here, we want young trained people... we'll be ready to welcome them at any time.' Sr St John Berchmans (Norrie O'Sullivan, Milltown, Co. Kerry) wrote to her sister in Drishane, Sr St Francis of Assisi (Nellie O'Sullivan) saying '... the harvest is indeed great. Are you coming out this year? My heart bleeds for all those coming out now, as it will mean a double sacrifice after having been some years in the Drishane Community... but where it is a question of heroism, the Irish are never behind.'[20]

After the War, the Sisters in Malaya were at pains to contact Ireland to tell them in Drishane how they had survived. Sr St Francis Xavier assured young novices that they were much needed in post-war Penang. She added that their teaching would be very much appreciated by the children who worked 'much more industriously than...children at home.' She continued:

> You may be sure that you will find many outlets to your zeal here. There is plenty of room for needlework and Cookery Mistresses and if you are artists you will not be idle. It is the solidarity that makes the happiness of Mission Life – the fact is that we all belong to a body which does much good, a lot of which is slow to show itself.[21]

Most significantly, Sr St Francis Xavier emphasised the particular purpose of mission life, which was the conversion to Christianity of the Chinese, and '...the building up of Christian homes due to Convent influence and the atmosphere of religion.'[22]

Sr St Francis Xavier's appeal did not fall on deaf ears, and as soon as the War was over, Drishane started to send Sisters again. During 1946, several Sisters went out including Sr St Martha (Mary Agatha Hickey, Ballingarry, Co. Limerick) who went to Kuala Lumpur; Sr St Danielle (Mary Horgan, Douglas, Cork) who went to Seremban; Sr St Cecile (Alice Butler, Ballyhennebry, Co. Kilkenny) and Sr St Angela (Enda Buckley, Cobh, Co. Cork) who both went to Singapore; Sr St Margaret Mary (Mary Corbett, Mallow, Co. Cork), who left for Malacca, and Sr St Alexis (Patricia O'Keeffe, Youghal, Co. Cork) who went to Penang. Their way had been paved by the very first post-war group to leave Drishane for the missions who departed for England on 31st July 1946, to join with some other sisters and continue the journey by sea to Singapore. This group comprised Sr St Bernardine (Mary Singleton, Cullen, Millstreet, Co. Cork), Sr St Rita (Ellen Murphy, Castleisland, Co. Kerry) and Sr St Xavier (Eilis Casey, Cork City).

THE FIRST VOYAGE OUT AFTER THE WAR: ONE ACCOUNT

There is a distinct sense of post-war optimism in the account of the journey undertaken by the first group of Drishane Sisters to go out to Singapore in 1946. Their journey is recorded in the Mission Annals, and is also documented in several letters that the Sisters sent home, giving us an unusually detailed account of this particular 'voyage out', and allowing us to

[20] Ibid.
[21] IJAD, Malaya Notebook, Malaysia-Singapore Collection.
[22] Ibid.

see many parts of this journey through the eyes of the travellers. From these documents, it is clear that the Irish Sisters enjoyed the adventures that the journey presented.[23] They first travelled from Drishane to Dublin, where they attended a Novena of Masses at the Dominican Church, before visiting an exhibition of Irish historical art. They were driven around Wicklow, Bray and Killiney by a Presentation brother, who managed to include a tour to the north side of the city that same day, in order to see the O'Connell monument and the grave of Michael Collins. Then the Sisters boarded a ship headed for Liverpool, but not before finding themselves at the centre of a small skirmish when striking dockers insisted on breaking their strike to carry the Sisters' trunks and luggage on board. This meant that the three Irish Sisters were invited to embark ahead of all of the passengers, and without even having to clear customs.

On arrival at Liverpool, the Sisters were met by Sr St Ita (Kate McSweeney, Crookstown, Co. Cork) and Mother St Patrick Enright, both of whom had travelled up from Weybridge. The next day, the intrepid Sisters embarked the *Empress of Scotland* which was scheduled to arrive in Singapore on the 21st August. They were delighted to find that all six of their party had been given a large cabin with six berths and so there was no need to share with strangers, as was customary at the time when sailing on former troop ships. The Sisters enjoyed sitting on deck, in chairs bought by Reverend Mother, who had anticipated that there might be a lack of luxury items on such a vessel. By 7th August they had passed Lisbon and sailed through the Straits of Gibraltar. The Sisters were enthralled by the sights of flying fish doing cartwheels on the water, and they marvelled at the beauty of the African coast, and the extraordinarily calm seas which they thought looked more like a lake. Each day the Sisters walked on deck, checking the ships' map where the officers marked the location of the vessel, and meeting Eurasian families who were travelling with children that were due to attend Infant Jesus schools in Malaya. On one occasion, Sr St Xavier Casey was approached by a little girl, who pointed out to sea and wondered aloud about a huge rock protruding from the water. Sr St Xavier explained it was 'an island'; the delighted child ran down the deck exclaiming aloud 'It's Ireland!' much to the horror of Sr St Xavier who feared her knowledge of geography would surely seem questionable among potential parents of Infant Jesus pupils.

By Sunday 14th August, the ship had entered Port Said, and the Sisters were able to watch the colourful and noisy markets and hard bargaining taking place in little vessels that came close to their ship. The Sisters had hoped to be allowed to go ashore to attend Mass, but there were no shore permits to be had. Because there was no priest travelling on the vessel, the Sisters badly wanted to hear Mass somewhere but the ship's Officer dismissed the request and advised them that they could conduct a 'divine service' in a room on board. The Sisters accepted the offer, and gathered a group of Catholic passengers together to pray.[24]

The next part of the journey must have been particularly significant for the Infant Jesus Sisters: they journeyed down the new Suez Canal, the construction of which had taken some 11,000 miles off the gruelling journey that their predecessors had made around the Cape to found convents in Malaya. Sailing on the Red Sea, Sr St Xavier commented that 'it was not red at all – it was as blue as the Mediterranean'. By 15th August, they had entered

[23] IJAD, Sr St Xavier to her family, 5th August 1946, in *Mission Annals, 1852-1945*.
[24] IJAD, Sr St Xavier to her family, 14th September 1946, in *Mission Annals, 1852-1945*.

the Indian Ocean, and the temperature dropped. When a severe gale blew up over two days, the Sisters strapped themselves into their bunks, excepting Sr St Xavier who 'dined alone' and did not feel the least bit seasick.[25] On 24th August, they arrived in Singapore harbour and marvelled at how like Ireland their surroundings seemed at first. They recorded:

> To our great joy, we espied the familiar habit on the pier. Six were waiting for us! Reverend Mother St Tarcisius, who is Regional Superior, had actually flown from Penang in the Governor's plane! We were so pleased she was here, that we felt quite at home immediately... a little after ten a.m. we disembarked... such a thrill first putting our foot on Malaya.[26]

Among the Irish Sisters awaiting the new arrivals at the Singapore convent was Sr St Elizabeth (Molly McSweeney, Farnanes, Co. Cork). Because of the War, the convent had not welcomed any new Sisters from Ireland for eight years, and this group was particularly welcome. Everything they saw in the first few days filled them with interest – such as how to negotiate the large convent grounds by day and how to use a mosquito net at night, and they were provided with quinine tablets to help prevent malaria. They also watched forty Japanese Prisoners of War who were helping to repair the damage done by the bombing.

WORK CONTINUES IN MALAYA/MALAYSIA

The three Irish Sisters who had arrived in Singapore in 1946 were given their obediences in late August. Sr St Xavier Casey went to Kuala Lumpur until 1948, at which time she moved to Seremban. Sr Rita Murphy went to Penang until 1949 when she moved to Taiping, and Sr St Bernardine Singleton remained in Singapore until 1953. The lives of these Irish Sisters were to change very considerably as they committed themselves to work very far from Ireland and different in almost every possible way. Sr St Xavier found the school at Kuala Lumpur was very large, with almost 2000 children. The primary school alone had eight or nine classes, all in the charge of Sr Finbarr Kennefick. Sr Finbarr had gone out to Kuala Lumpur from Drishane in 1915, as one of the first missionaries to leave from the Novitiate. Pupils in the school were Chinese, Indian, Tamil, Malay, and Eurasian, and few of these were Catholic.

The Sisters in Malaya were kept busy teaching in their schools. Writing to Drishane from Ipoh in September 1946, Sr St Cecile Butler told about her new life on the missions:

> For the first week, I helped here and there, but now my time-table is fixed. I have some subjects with St[andard] VII and VIII; the work is mostly on the Oxford Syllabus, so I am not entirely a stranger to it, T.G. We start school at 8 o'clock and finish at one... I am with the boarders too, every morning for breakfast and every second night for study and recreation... the first Sunday night they gave me a concert.[27]

Sr St Cecile, like Sr St Francis Xavier in Kuala Lumpur, encouraged the Drishane Sisters to come out to Malaya to help in the schools:

> As I said to you that day in the train at Mallow, wherever we go, it is home, and I must say I have found a second home in Ipoh. I only wish I could go back to Drishane and bring another

---

[25] IJAD, Sr St Xavier to her family, 18th September 1946, in *Mission Annals, 1852-1945*.
[26] IJAD, *Mission Annals, 1852-1945*.
[27] IJAD, Sr St Cecile to Drishane, September 1946, in *Mission Annals, 1852-1945*.

dozen back with me; there is so much work to be done, "the harvest indeed is great, but the labourers are few".[28]

Drishane responded by supplying new labourers for the harvest in the late 1940s and early 1950s. In 1947, Sr St Francis de Sales (Julia Sheehan, Templeglantine, Co Limerick) went to Penang, and Sr St Lawrence Tarrant went to Malacca. In 1949, Sr St John Bosco (Elizabeth O'Riordan, Patrickswell, Co Limerick) went to Kuala Lumpur, where she began a mission that continued until 1985. Kuala Lumpur was also the destination for Sr St Canice (Ita Higgins, Youghal, Co Cork) that year, and she remained in Malaya for twenty years.

Mission Sisters were not the only people at the Malayan convents to communicate with Drishane. Pupils at the schools were encouraged by Irish Sisters to write letters to tell the Drishane girls about their lives, and in December 1947 one of Sr St Cecile's pupils, Chai-Mi-Lan, wrote to tell about her education in Ipoh. The school at that time had nearly 2000 pupils, comprising Chinese, Indian, English and Eurasian girls. 'In spite of the differences of race and creed,' she wrote, 'we all get on very well together.' She continued to describe school life, concluding with a vivid account of a December 'sale of work' that the school was planning. In many details, the sale resembled accounts of the bi-annual sale held at Drishane and the various fund-raising sales that the Sisters co-ordinated at many of their schools. In addition to knitting clothes for the sale, the pupils had made toffee and biscuits, and had gathered raffle prizes such as dolls and a bicycle. The most attractive item to be raffled, however, was a motorbike, for which the girls had sold a thousand raffle tickets. 'The appearance of the motor-cycle created a sensation', Chai-Mi-Lan wrote. 'It is indeed an extraordinary machine, without pedals, evidently a new model and specially suited for a lady.'[29]

The work of the Sisters in Malaya/Malaysia has been acknowledged in many private and public expressions of gratitude. For example, in 1936 Reverend Mother St Tarcisius was awarded an OBE for her services to education and charity in Malaysia. At the award ceremony, the chairman of the Old Girls' Association gave an address which was published in the *Straits Echo,* in which she said:

> The Penang Convent has educated in a true sense of the word, several generations and it has made them useful citizens... within the hallowed walls of the Convent, our mothers, ourselves and our children have received and are still receiving that complete form of education, which includes not only physical and intellectual, but also sound moral training.[30]

In 1946, further public recognition of the work of the Sisters came. The Resident Commissioner of Kuala Lumpur, on behalf of the Government, presented thirty Certificates of Commendation to individuals for services to the people of Malaya during the War. Included in the list of recipients were three Infant Jesus Sisters at Kuala Lumpur: Reverend Mother St Adele, Reverend Mother St Martha (Margaret Kelleher, Millstreet, Co. Cork), and Sr St Margaret (Jane Elgin, Scotland). On the day of the presentations, Reverend Mother St Adele refused to attend, saying that she was 'too busy looking after her children', but the Resident Commissioner was not to be deterred: he arrived at the convent on the 12th September to make the presentation in front of the Sisters and children.[31]

---

[28] Ibid.
[29] IJAD, Chai-Mi-Lan to Drishane, 2nd December 1947, in *Mission Annals, 1852-1945.*
[30] A C Reutens, address on the occasion of the award of the OBE to Reverend Mother St Tarcisius, Penang, 1936. Quoted in Yap, *The Convent Light Street,* 79.
[31] IJAD, Sr St Xavier to her family, in *Mission Annals, 1852-1945.*

The many records of thanks to the Sisters include those of their past pupils who have often commented on the stamina of the seemingly tireless Sisters. For example, the energy of Sr St Francis de Sales Sheehan, whose mission to Malaya/Malaysia lasted from 1947 until her death in 1998, has been noted by Dilys Yap. Having taught at the Convent Light Street from 1947 to 1962, Sr St Francis de Sales then went to the Convent in Johore Baru. Between 1964 and 1965 she worked in Singapore, and then returned to Convent Light Street to become Principal until her retirement in 1978. After that, as one past-pupil recalled: '... she worked tirelessly to raise funds...she sat at the [convent] front gate in her wheel chair greeting old pupils and friends... the students found her strict but always went to her for advice.'[32]

Sr St Francis de Sales had travelled out to her mission with Sr St Damien (Peggy Murphy, Crookstown, Co. Cork). Sr St Damien taught in Singapore from 1947 until 1954, after which she went to Penang. She returned to Singapore in 1954, and with the exception of a short time in Johore Bahru, she remained in Singapore until 1983. In her thirty-seven years in Singapore, during which time it had become part of the Federation of Malaya (1963) and then become an independent republic (1965), Sr Damien (Peggy) witnessed many changes not only in Singapore but also in the way that 'mission' was understood. Reflecting on the start of her life there she said:

> It was just after the War, the heat was terrible, the relics of war were around... it was a culture shock... and it was tough, the heat, and the cockroaches were dreadful... [but] we loved going in to those little children... I was teaching from the day I arrived, up at 5.30, then meditation, then office, then Mass, then breakfast, then school. After school, back to your drawing board to correct mountains of books. [We had] ... no discipline problems, the pupils were so thirsty to learn... I thought we were going out to convert, that we were bringing the good news – but they had the good news, Christ was already with them, it was enabling them to discover Him for themselves rather than teaching them catechism.[33]

Another Irish Sister whose mission to Malaya spanned the second half of the twentieth century was Sr St Aidan (Margaret Fitzgerald, Bandon, Co. Cork). She had four aunts in the Institute, two of them in Malaya, Sr St Thomas and Sr St Andrew. Sr St Aidan was sent to Penang in 1954, having graduated from University College Cork. While in Drishane, she was influenced by missionary Sisters who were home visiting, and she was also influenced by Mother St Albert who would read letters from Malaya to the novices. Sr St Aidan went out to teach Science and English at Convent Light Street until 1968, when she moved to Green Lane Convent. She became Principal there in 1972, taking over from Sr St Helen O'Sullivan who had been there from its foundation. Reflecting on her time on the missions, Sr Aidan said that the 'Drishane welcome' and the 'good start' that Sr St Helen gave to Green Lane created a 'sense of belonging'. As Sr Aidan continued, the work of Sr Helen was like that of Mother Claire Bringeon who founded Drishane: 'The pupils always had that sense of belonging to a group and I hope that will continue. I think the founder always leaves a spirit that carries on.'[34] Commenting on the legacy of the Infant Jesus Sisters in Malaysia, Sr Aidan believes that part of their gift to their pupils was 'a bit of the Irish discipline':

> ... a few [past pupils] have said to me, especially when they had hard knocks in life, 'thank you for the discipline you taught me, otherwise I couldn't have borne up under it'...

---

[32] Yap, *The Convent Light Street*, 82.
[33] Sr Peggy Murphy, interview with the authors, 16th July, 2008.
[34] Sr Aidan Fitzgerald, interview with the authors, 15th July, 2008.

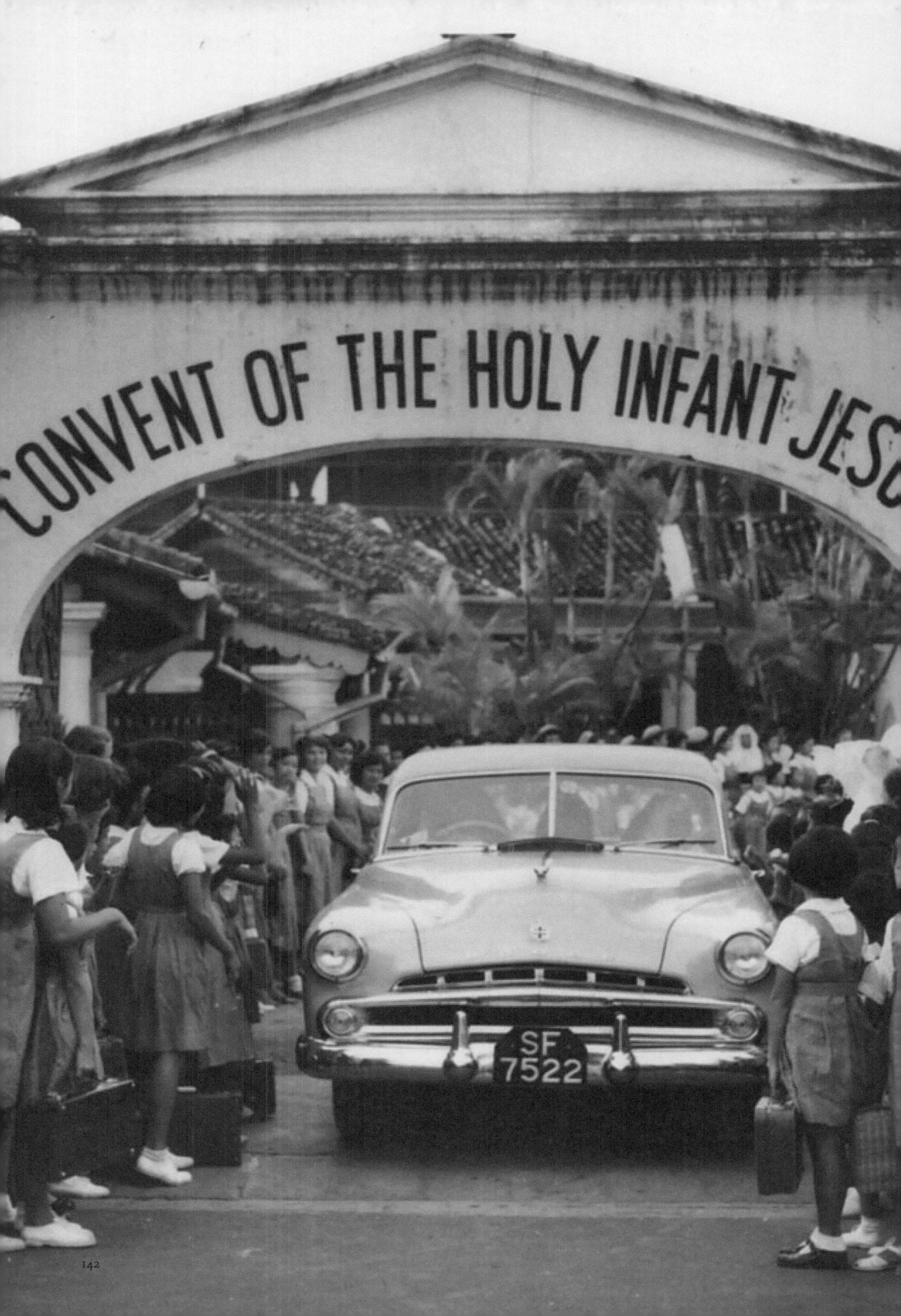
CONVENT OF THE HOLY INFANT JESU
SF
7522

Opposite: Mother St Charles'
car leaving Singapore, 1955

Above: Sr Aidan Fitzgerald
with her aunt Sr Andrew
Fitzgerald

Below: Singapore 1965, Sr St Elizabeth Browne with her pupils including
on left, Theresa Lee (on the staff at that time and now a Sister) and centre
(with dark-rimmed glasses) Maria Lau now Provinicial Superior

> We shared Christian values that were appreciated by all faiths... it's the atmosphere of love
> and faith that you create as a body, [and] not just the person who instructs.'[35]

The Sisters also provided rigorous teaching, and while many of them could teach English with ease, there were curricular demands that challenged them at intervals. Sr Nellie O'Sullivan recalled, with good humour, being asked to teach A Level history in Malaysia:

> I thought I was the cat's pyjamas in history until I was shown the syllabus. All the history I
> had learned was European but this was Asian history. And there was hardly a book to be
> had! We worked so hard, I got everything possible, so that before the year was out we had
> covered the syllabus in history. China and Japan. You just had to do it... We worked so hard.
> And every time they write, [they say] how grateful they are for what we brought them...[36]

The Convent Light Street, like other Malaysian convents, changed in the second half of the twentieth century and the Government took over the administration of the school in 1958. After the mid-1960s, the Convent no longer accepted babies, and the boarding section of the school was discontinued. In 1989, the last of the orphans with disabilities were brought to Bukit Nanas, in Kuala Lumpur, and parts of the old buildings were pulled down. Today, the Convent Light Street has both a primary and secondary school and, like many of the Infant Jesus Convent schools, it retains some of its original ethos while responding to new and changing demands.

This retention of the original ethos, or 'spirit', in Singapore has also been commented upon by Sr St Elizabeth (Browne, Rockchapel, Co. Cork) who was there from 1954 until 1982, and she notes that the teachers, pupils and parents attached to the school were appreciative of the Infant Jesus legacy and have not forgotten it:

> They wanted their children to be educated, and they thank us for that... They were our friends,
> and they thank us for being their friends... for the IJ spirit, it was love and compassion and
> consideration for others. This teacher told me that when the new pupils come in every year
> she takes them on a trip to Victoria Street and shows them all around. They have kept it all,
> the convent is still there, even our community room: *marche dans ma présence et sois parfait!*
> It is still up there. She takes them back there to get the IJ spirit.[37]

Sr Hannah (Anne Marie Murray, The Lough, Cork) was the last of the Infant Jesus Sisters to go to Malaysia in 1967. Because of the political situation, it proved impossible to get a visa to allow her to continue teaching, so in 1972 she left for a new mission in Melbourne, Australia.

WORK CONTINUES IN JAPAN

In much the same way that Drishane had quickly sent Sisters to Malaya after the War ended, it also responded to the needs of its convents in Japan in the second half of the twentieth century. In 1946, Sr St Joan of Arc (Joan Twomey, Whitechurch, Co. Cork) went to Yokohama and in 1948, Sr St Odile (Kathleen O'Sullivan, Doneraile, Co. Cork) went to Yokohama. The newcomers in Japan, like those in Malaya, always felt close to Drishane.

---

[35] Ibid.
[36] Sr Nellie O'Sullivan, interview with the authors, 15th July, 2008.
[37] Sr Elizabeth Browne, interview with the authors, 15th July, 2008.

Indeed it is striking to see how often they referred very affectionately to Drishane, and to other Drishane Sisters, in their letters. For example, when Sr St Marie Noël (Scanlan, Sunday's Well, Cork) wrote back to Ireland upon her arrival in Singapore, and later in Yokohama, her letters indicated the warm welcome that awaited her, Sr St Senan (Catherine Fitzgerald, Liscarroll, Co. Cork), and Sr St Odile, in both places. As their ship neared Singapore, they spotted the welcome party:

> ... Lo! Four black coiffes could be seen and a dazzling white bonnet and fichu at some distance on the quayside. What a moment that was! Out came the handkerchiefs and ere long we could recognise Sr St Josephine (Kathleen Boland, Ardfert, Co. Kerry), nearly dancing the Kerry Dance with joy. Next Sr St Alexis O'Keeffe... Mother St Charles, Sr St Paul and Sr Hermione.[38]

Later, at the Convent in Singapore, other Drishane Sisters came to welcome them and to get news of Drishane. Sr St Bernardine, and Sr St John greeted them, as did Sr St Aidan, Sr St Simon (Julia Duffy, Rathclooney, Co. Clare), and Sr St Benedict O'Connell. 'How kind they are and how they plied us with questions about Drishane', Sr St Marie Noël wrote, concluding: 'Then a high supper... and so to bed! This ceremony, with all the attendant kindness and attention of our Sisters St Damien, Angela, Josephine and Finbarr, made me dream I was once again back in the Novitiate, October 23rd, 1945, a budding postulant whose *petit couché* was attended with such kindness.'

After a brief visit in Singapore, the Sisters continued their long sea voyage to Japan and they arrived one month later in Yokohama, where they would be given their obediences. Sr St Marie Noël again wrote to Drishane to tell of the welcome that awaited the newcomers. The Irish Sisters who came on board their ship, the *Glencairn*, to greet them included Mother St Enda Fitzgerald, Sr St Joan of Arc, Sr St Veronica, Sr St Virgilius, Sr Sr Lelia, and Sr St Joseph. Perhaps not surprisingly, Sr St Marie Noël noted that the lounge on the Glencairn 'was like a Convent parlour.'[39]   The Sisters were then transported to the convent in Yokohama, and later in the day, other Irish Sisters came to the convent from Tokyo to welcome the new arrivals: Sr St Columba O'Donoghue, Sr St Teresita Dwyer and Sr St Paul of the Cross (Elizabeth Casey, Brosna, Co. Kerry). And in the evening Mother St Eugene and Sr St Senan arrived to make them feel even more at home. After prayers they were given a superb feast, about which Sr St Marie Noël wrote to Reverend Mother at Drishane in a lengthy letter:

> No need to tell you we did full justice to the feast, while you and Drishane and each and everyone in it, with special mention of Sr St Mary Magdalen, Sr St James, and Sr St Teresa, was the exhaustless topic of conversation. Indeed so impregnated was the air with Drishane and with the familiar faces about us that it was hard not to dream at odd moments that one was back there... It was a lovely surprise to find that some of Sr St Stanislaus's seeds had travelled with us, so now we shall see a spot of Drishane blooming on the Bluff.[40]

Activity at the Infant Jesus schools in Japan was similar to that in Malaya. Writing in 1948 a year after she had arrived in Yokohama from Drishane, Sr St Carmel (Eileen O'Keeffe, Cobh, Co. Cork) told the Sisters at home about her new life:

> School has not closed yet and like yourselves we have a busy week before us - tests, marks, plays, etc. Since St Maur [International School] opened I am just dazed. There is not even

---

[38] IJAD, Sr St Marie Noël to Reverend Mother St Anthony, 1st February 1949.
[39] Ibid.
[40] Ibid.

> time to die here! ...our building is going ahead. At the moment a beautiful auditorium is
> coming into shape...you will wonder where Reverend Mother is getting the money for such
> ventures – well it seems to come in instalments from nowhere![41]

In reality, Reverend Mother managed to raise funds for the school in Yokohama by doing
exactly what the Sisters in Drishane and Malaya did: they held bazaars and sales of work.
Sr St Carmel commented jokingly that life at Yokohama was like 'a continued sale', and the
Sisters worked in their spare time at the 'brisk business' of remaking old clothes that had
been donated by 'kind Americans' in order to sell them at the sales of work.

Life for the Sisters in Yokohama followed a routine:

> ...at 5.30 am the bell summons us from the land of nod. Mass is at 6.30, breakfast at 7.15 and
> the day's work of teaching begins at 7.45 am in the Japanese school and continues until 4pm.
> Since the International School opened there is not time to breathe... 8.30 each morning
> sees me speeding over to the new building. Fifth and sixth grades are a mixture of Germans,
> French, Turks, Russians, Chinese, Americans, Japanese and Filipinos.[42]

Pleasant entertainment was provided when the Sisters took their pupils to plays, such as
a production of *The Song of Bernadette* at the Sacred Heart University, and *Scrooge* at St
Joseph's College. The Sisters also enjoyed occasional visits from Irish relatives who were in
the area, such as Fr O'Donovan, the brother of Sr St John Berchmans, who visited Yokohama
twice in 1948, bringing 'great accounts' of a recent visit he had made to Drishane. And at
intervals the Sisters also had to cope with the vagaries of the climate. On the night of 31st
August 1949 the typhoon 'Kitty' came up over Yokohama and one gable end of the convent
was completely blown down. The chimneys and railings were also swept away, and tiles
flew from the roof. The rains that followed caused flooding in the convent, and the Sisters
soon found themselves putting out buckets to catch the leaks and mopping furiously. Sr St
Marie Noël recreated the scene with good humour:

> Walt Disney would have done a prize-worthy cartoon, could he have had a peep both at the
> moppers and the flooded rooms! I leave our attire to your imagination while I describe the
> floors. The water kept coming in through the ceiling... so to meet such an emergency we
> had every variety of container placed to catch the fall... tubs, buckets, pails, baking tins,
> kettles, tea pots...the mopping and emptying of receptacles was quite a business... [43]

The rains stopped the following day, and the damage was repaired. Shortly after, with
the return of the heat and sunshine, the Sisters began to go in relays for their holiday
at Akobara. There they could enjoy the cool of the hills. Sr St Marie Noël recalled that
they would remove the sliding panels of the side of their holiday house, to allow the fresh
breezes to blow through, and they would enjoy the beauty that surrounded them:

> Sometimes we took picnic meals up in the hills, or else had early suppers and took up
> cushions and sat on a high spot overlooking the bay and the surrounding country till bedtime,
> going homeward to the accompanying scenes of the most gorgeous sunsets you could conceive,
> and the strains of a constant orchestra, which charms night and day... from every variety of
> bird and insect.[44]

---

[41] IJAD, Sr St Carmel to Drishane, December 1946, in *Mission Annals 1852-1945*.
[42] Ibid.
[43] IJAD, Sr St Marie Noël to Drishane, 29th August 1949, in *Mission Annals, 1852-1945*.
[44] Ibid.

Although the Sisters were very busy, they were uplifted by their work, and Sr St Carmel wrote to Ireland: 'You are probably waiting to hear how life in Yokohama is agreeing with me. Well, it is all that I have ever wished for, each day seems to find me happier.'[45] Drishane was never far from the thoughts of the Sisters, as is clear from constant references to it in the letters and Annals of the Sisters. As Sr St Marie Noël wrote from Yokohama in 1949:

> We had Sr St Columba with us in Yokohama for some weeks, and while she was with us she, Sr St Carmel, Sr St Joan, Sr St Odile and I had a walk together at Akobara... how often Drishane came into our chats as we gossiped away on our perch on the hill when the heat of the day had passed, gazing at the beauty beyond and beneath, and all agreeing we had indeed the hundred-fold and wishing those near to us could have a peep.[46]

The work of the Sisters also continued at the convent at Fukuoka. Sr St Christopher Lyne, who had survived internment, continued her mission there. She was joined in 1947 by Sr St Maureen (Roddy, Derry), and over a period of three or four years the junior and senior schools were rebuilt despite the difficulty of getting good building materials after the War. Sr St Maureen wrote back to Drishane in 1950, to tell of the success at Fukuoka which had enrolled five hundred senior pupils in the fine new building that year.[47] Other Drishane Sisters who went to Japan in the second half of the twentieth century were Sr St Agatha (Ahern, Magazine Road, Cork City), Sr St Columban (Ann Breen, Castletownbere, Co. Cork) and Sr St Clare O'Callaghan. Sr Agatha recalled: 'We were eighteen Sisters left Marseilles in 1952; sixteen stayed in Malaysia-Singapore and two went on to Japan, a French Sister and myself.'[48] Sr Agatha had entered the Novitiate in 1944 having been a pupil at Drishane. She was influenced in her decision to enter by Sr St Mary Murphy O'Connor, and after her first profession she went to France and later to Roehampton to do teacher training. While in France she had spoken with Mother General Jean Desmet, who told her that she would be going to Malaya, and then added, 'Je me suis trompée. I meant Japan'. Sr Agatha continued:

> We went out by ship...[the journey] was about five or six weeks. And, of course, it was interesting because we saw all these places, Djibouti and Manila and Saigon... It was straight after the War and I never remember being deprived of anything... Sr St Enda Fitzgerald was very much involved in the new building which was convent and school at that time. We were in the same grounds as Futaba... it was a nice convent, the school was downstairs and we were upstairs... We loved Japan and we fitted in very well with the Japanese... we were all one, we were quite a big Community.[49]

Sr Clare O'Callaghan, who went to Japan a little later (1961), had entered the Drishane Novitiate with a large group: 'A whole bunch of us entered at that time, Gertie Lalor, Catherine Shanahan, Réidín Scannell, Nora Hartnett, Catherine O'Sullivan...' Reflecting on her mission she recalled: '... the Japanese Provincial at the time, Mother Emmanuel, came to Ireland looking for Sisters who would be willing to teach English... straight away I put my name forward.'[50] Mother Emmanuel asked for a commitment of only three years, but Sr Clare chose to make Japan her mission and stayed until 2008:

---

[45] IJAD, Sr St Carmel to Drishane, in *Mission Annals 1852-1945*.
[46] IJAD, Sr St Marie Noël to Drishane, 29th August 1949, in *Mission Annals, 1852-1945*.
[47] IJAD, Sr St Maureen to Drishane, Autumn 1950, in *Mission Annals, 1852-1945*.
[48] Sr Agatha Ahern, interview with the authors, 15th July 2008.
[49] Ibid.
[50] Sr Clare O'Callaghan, interview with the authors, 15th July 2008.

Opposite: Fukuoka, c. 1968.
L to R: Sr Maureen Roddy, Sr Francis Xavier
O'Shea, Mother General Justin.

Above: Yokohama, 1961. Sr St Agatha
Ahern and her pupils.

...so a three-year contract, and I lasted forty-six. And I got more for my faith in Japan than I got anywhere... I went out full of zeal, full of fervour and I was going to spread the message of God to these people... But it was I got it all from them... I got more than I could ever, ever imagine. I was the one who was converted... What did I do for the past 46 years? I did nothing. But so many came to thank me for what they got for their lives... they all come to us when they are broken, they could come to the Sisters and say all they wanted to say and know it would stay there. And that was something. But I didn't do anything. It was the Holy Spirit.[51]

THE INSTITUTE IN THAILAND

As early as 1885, at the request of the Apostolic Vicar of Thailand, the Infant Jesus Sisters had been invited to open a convent in Bangkok. Among the first Sisters to go there was the Irishwoman, Sr St Veronica (Kitty Parker, Limerick) who arrived from her mission in Singapore in 1888. In 1895, Sr St Agnes (Mary Duggan, Balbriggan, Co. Dublin) and Sr St Elizabeth (Barry, Limerick) went out, and they were joined by Sr St Norbert Hare in 1900.

Other Sisters, such as Sr St Ursula (Nora Murphy, Ballywalter, Co. Wicklow) and Sr St Alban (Mary Neylon, Co. Clare) who also went to Bangkok in 1900, Sr St Marcienne (Sarah McGann, Ennis, Co. Clare) who went in 1901, and Sr St Egbert (Mary Galvin, Kilnamona, Toureen, Co. Clare) who went in 1906, all worked hard to build the Thai mission. However, it struggled in part because people were wary about entrusting their children to religious, as they did not know about them, and in part because of repeated outbreaks of cholera. Five young Sisters, including Sr St Elizabeth from Limerick, died there before 1907 at which time the school was handed over to another order, the Sisters of St Paul de Chartres.

The Infant Jesus Sisters were to return to Thailand and take over the Bangkok convent again in 1957. Mother St Charles and five Sisters began once again the mission in Bangkok, arriving there on 16th February to a welcome from the Bishop and priests of the diocese, and many friends.

Sisters who went out to Thailand in the 1960s and 1970s included Sr St Martha Hickey and Sr St Marie (Eileen Conheady, Newmarket-on-Fergus, Co. Clare), while Sr St Mary (Margaret Mary Lunt, Liverpool) was there from as early as 1958 when she went to Bangkok from her mission in Penang. She had gone out to Penang in 1936, and had survived internment during the War. In the decades that followed, she had worked in both Kuala Lumpur and Singapore, and then in 1950 she was asked to return to Liverpool to open a house for Sisters from Malaysia who were studying in England. In 1952 she returned to Malaysia, and then in 1958 she was asked to go to Thailand. Though she was reluctant to leave Malaysia, which she loved greatly, she accepted the challenge ahead. She and Sr Jerome, a Thai Sister, together with the Redemptorists, founded a village for leper families at Non Sombun, near Khan Kaen, with its own church and school. Sr Mary spent twenty years there. When Sr Mary finally left Thailand for England in 1978, she did not retire

---

[51] Ibid.

from work: she found a new apostolate in East Acton, visiting the inmates at Wormwood
Scrubs Prison. There she taught English, and was a catechist attached to the chaplaincy
until her retirement to live with the Weybridge community in 1988. Following the closure
of Weybridge in 1997, Sr Mary moved to Mallow and she died peacefully in 2001 at the age
of 96. She is buried in Drishane.

Above: Sr Mary Lunt at Non Sombun.

THE IRISH MISSION TO THE USA

Just as the 1950s saw the Institute grow in Thailand, it also saw the Infant Jesus Sisters arrive in the USA to establish their first American foundation. The Archbishop of San Francisco, Most Reverend John J Mitty, sent Fr Mark Hurley to Drishane to meet with one of his relatives, Mother St Anthony Coleman, with a view to seeing if Sisters could be spared to open a convent and school in Healdsburg, in the Archdiocese of San Francisco. Five Sisters, Sr Ann Crowley, Sr Helen (Mary Helen Keane, Ballylongford, Co. Kerry), Sr St Thomas Aquinas (Geraldine Forde, Boherbue, Co. Cork), Sr St Fintan (Margaret McAuliffe, Lixnaw, Co.Kerry) and Sr St Marie Noël Scanlan (*via* Japan), were among the founding group. The Sisters were temporarily hosted by the Ursuline Sisters in Santa Rosa, until their convent and school (St John the Baptist's) was ready. At an early stage, Mother St Thomas Aquinas learned that schooling in the USA was co-educational, and they contacted Mother General Jean Desmet to ask how they should proceed. It is recorded that she advised by telegram that they should 'Follow the customs of the country', and the Sisters opened a primary school for boys and girls, including non-Catholic children. The Institute in the USA would grow over the years, opening a convent and school (Holy Angels) at Colma, and another convent and school (St Veronica's) in South San Francisco.

Shortly after their arrival in the USA, Reverend Mother St Thomas Aquinas and the Healdsburg community were visited by Tim Daly, a local man who had originally come from Reverend Mother's home town in Co Cork. He befriended the community, and secured the support of a few of his Irish friends to help with tasks that needed to be undertaken at the new convent. The band of volunteers named themselves the Drishane Club. They were mostly Irish people, who had come to the USA, and they supported the Healdsburg Community through fundraising and providing practical help to the Sisters such as building fences around the Healdsburg convent grounds, and facilitating the purchase of a new car for the Sisters. When the Infant Jesus Sisters opened a foundation at Colma, the Drishane Club extended their help to this new community too. The Drishane Club is mentioned regularly in the Annals, and in 1953 the convent annalist noted: 'the Drishane Club deserves to be remembered and ranked high among [our] early benefactors.[52]

When it was decided to have a second foundation in Colma, Reverend Mother St Thomas Aquinas was sent to lead the new community which comprised Sr St Regis (Nellie Fitzgerald, Ballylanders, Co. Limerick), Sr St Thomas More (Cecilia Cronin, Cobh, Co. Cork), Sr St Hilary (Mary O'Rourke, Newmarket-on-Fergus, Co. Clare) and Sr St Attracta (Evelyn Houlihan, Kilmallock, Co. Limerick). The Sisters were given great support for the foundation by their Pastor, Fr Morrissey, who remained a friend to them until his untimely death in 1954. The Sisters were also warmly welcomed by the people of Colma, who were delighted to have a new Catholic school. In September 1952, the Infant Jesus Sisters conducted their first full day of school at Holy Angels. The day was described by Reverend Mother St Thomas Aquinas in a letter back to Drishane:

> Colma opened on September 10th. On that morning the children assembled on the playground, and teachers, parents and pupils knelt for Fr Morrissey's blessing before beginning work. We have five grades, fifty in each grade, almost as many more had to be refused admittance for want of teachers... all the parents are clamouring for Christian education for their children.

---

52 IJAD, 21st June 1953, *Colma Mission Annals.*

Already seventy of those who cannot come to us have registered for Catechism classes outside school hours...please ask all the Crusaders and especially Tig Bríde in the B[oarding] S[chool] and the technical school to remember Healdsburg and Colma in their prayers and sacrifices... Both school and convent are very well equipped and are supposed to be the most beautiful of their kind in the Archdiocese... I only wish you could see the fittings and the colour schemes. God grant that the work done for souls will be equally perfect.[53]

In the early months of this foundation, the people of Colma demonstrated their warm regard for the Sisters through many generous gestures, such as sending flowers each week for the chapel altar, supplying bread, cakes and fruit for the kitchen, and providing carpets and furniture for the convent and school. They also gave each of the Sisters a 'sturdy umbrella', in preparation for the occasional heavy rainfall! Members of the Drishane Club showed the Sisters around their new town, and drove them to appointments and to visit the community at Healdsburg. The waiting list for entry to the Holy Angels School grew long, and its reputation spread as parents began to see the high standard of teaching and examining that the Sisters demonstrated. Sr Pauline O'Dwyer, who became Superior at Colma and Principal of Holy Angels in 1972, recalled that 'there was a very good spirit at Holy Angels'; the school succeeded in 'building up learning' rather than just teaching the curriculum, and as a consequence many of their pupils were accepted into the High Schools of their preference and did not find the transition to High School too difficult.

On 19th April 1953, the Colma foundation was officially opened. The planning for the day had been undertaken by the Sisters and their many new friends, including the members of the Mothers' Guild. The Annals record that new benches arrived in time to be installed in the chapel; there was also new flagstone for a patio on which a statue of Our Lady of Fatima, delivered from Italy, was placed. A ceremony was planned to take place out of doors in the California sunshine, and a special platform was built on which the 'dignitaries' were to be seated. The day dawned bringing relentless rain, so the Sisters' plans had to be changed quickly, and the ceremony was moved to the church. The Archbishop, Most Reverend John J Mitty, officiated and 'colour was added by a group of Knights of Columbus and a Highland Fife and Drum band.'[54]

By 1954, the community at Colma had grown with the arrival of Sr St Henry (Elizabeth Golden, Magazine Road, Cork), Sr St Louise (Kathleen Roche, Mallow, Co. Cork) and Sr St Leo (Mary Cotter, Doneraile, Co. Cork) and while Sr St Regis left for Weybridge in 1955, the community still 'reached the magical number of eight – one Sister for every class group in the school' – when Sr St Maria Goretti (Mary Kiely, Garbally, Co. Tipperary) arrived.

The two Communities were only about eighty miles apart so there was constant contact between the Sisters at Healdsburg and Colma. As Sr Pauline has noted, the Infant Jesus Sisters 'were a small group in a large country, so the contact was important'. The two Communities spent Christmas together, and the Sisters enjoyed annual holidays at a house on Dillon Beach. In letters to Drishane, the Sisters said that Dillon Beach reminded them of Ballyferriter. There was also regular contact with Drishane, and the arrival of additional Sisters was recorded carefully in the Annals.

---

[53] IJAD, Reverend Mother St Thomas Aquinas to Drishane, 10th September 1952, *Mission Annals, 1951-1955.*
[54] IJAD, 19th April 1953, *Colma Mission Annals.*

California, 1964. Front L to R: Sr Hilary O'Rourke, Sr Helen Keane, Sr Cecilia Cronin, Sr Thomas Aquinas Forde, Sr Consilia Quinn, Sr Evelyn Houlihan, Sr Mary Jo Murray, Sr Beatrice Ahern. Middle L to R: Sr Pat Condon, Sr Maryann Nolan, Sr Fintan McAuliffe, Sr Mary Cotter, Sr Margaret Cotter, Sr Elizabeth Golden, Sr Monica Dunne, Sr Pauline O'Dwyer, Sr Louise Roche. Back L to R: Sr Lally Moriarty, Sr Barbara Balbi, Sr Kathleen O'Sullivan, Sr Ann Crowley, Sr Rosario McAuliffe, Sr Mary Madden.

Many American features of the social side of school life were adopted by the Sisters at Healdsburg and Colma. They ran 'hot-dog sales' in place of cake sales, and when Spring came, preparations for First Holy Communion included a 'Fathers and Daughters' breakfast. The Sisters also enjoyed the celebrations for St Valentine's Day when the mothers baked special cakes and held a party at the school where the children exchanged Valentine cards. And the Sisters also brought features of their Drishane education to the USA. With their pupils they organised musical events, staged operettas, and held folk dancing festivals that drew praise from the parents who were very involved in supporting the Sisters.

The late 1950s was a period of rapid change in society and within the Institute and innovations in technology had an impact on the Communities. The aeroplane had replaced the liner as the mode of transport to the USA missions, so while the Cotter twins, Sr St Eugenie and Sr St Leo, had arrived from Drishane via the liner from Cobh to New York in 1953, by 1955 the Sisters could fly in and out from the new San Francisco International Airport, via Paris/New York. In 1956, the Sisters were presented with their first television set. A gift from the Drishane Club, the television was used by the Sisters to follow a course called 'Shakespeare on TV', and early in 1957 five of the Sisters took an examination on the course, held at the University of San Francisco. When summer came, a group of ten Sisters from the Colma and Healdsburg communities enrolled for a six-week course at the University of San Francisco. Many of the first Sisters who went to the USA had gone out before having the opportunity for higher education or degrees. As it was necessary to have a Californian teaching qualification in order to teach at the schools, the Sisters were keen to pursue their studies. Over many years, and during their annual summer holidays, the Sisters took subjects for credits at the USF, leading to the award of degrees and teaching diplomas.

In 1958, the community was visited by Fr Coleman, the Pastor of St Veronica's parish, in San Mateo County. He asked for some Sisters to start a much-needed school. The Sisters were aware that many children at the Holy Angels belonged to Fr Coleman's parish, and had heard their parents lament the absence of a local Catholic school. On St Patrick's Day, news came from Mother General in Paris that the Sisters could take the offer of the school. Sr St Thomas More from Colma and Sr St Beatrice (Catherine Ahern, Magazine Road, Cork) from Healdsburg started St Veronica's school in September 1958. This was a year in which Sr St Fintan arrived back from Ireland accompanied by two young Sisters from Drishane to increase the presence of the Institute in the USA. They were Sr St Rosario (Margaret McAuliffe, Cobh, Co Cork), and Sr St Monica (Mary Dunne, Bunavoy, Old Pallas, Limerick). Sr St Fintan's mission to the USA lasted from 1950 to 1985, during which time she was central to the running of the Healdburg convent; she also had an outward mission to the people of Healdsbrug. They presented her with an award for her services to Healdsburg on her retirement, and named after her a building, Fintan Hall.

In June of 1959, the Sisters in the USA suffered the loss of Sr St Oliver Moore, who was a devoted teacher at Healdsburg. She had come to the USA in 1956, after studying at University College Cork. She is the only Infant Jesus Sister buried in the USA, having been laid to rest in Holy Cross Cemetery, South San Francisco. The memory of Sr St Oliver was honoured in 1960, when the first postulant from California, Pat Condon (originally from

Liverpool), was received. The Annals recorded with delight: 'A big day for Colma... Sr Pat Condon, is to be received today. What will she be called?' A few days later the Annals note that she will 'henceforth be called Sr St Oliver. Sr St Oliver Moore wasted no time in getting herself replaced'.[55]

In October of that year, there was much interest in the presidential election, and on November 9th the Sisters recorded:

> Everybody foresaw a close election, but it was even closer than expected. After considerable stress and strain and waiting, the final victory goes to John Fitzgerald Kennedy. The *Monitor* tells us that Catholics can now tear up their 'second class citizen' certificates as the Catholic has at last 'arrived'. Now, for added reasons, Catholics have a duty to pray for the President. This is being called the golden age of the Catholic laity. Would that our President may be one of its shining lights. Deo Volente! [56]

On 20th January 1961, the Sisters recorded that pupils brought television sets to school to set up in each classroom, so that all could watch the inauguration of John F. Kennedy, 'first Catholic President of the United States'.[57]

The 1960s were to bring more changes for the Sisters in the USA. Early in 1961, after nine years as Superior at Colma, Reverend Mother St Thomas Aquinas returned once more to Healdsburg as Superior, and Mother St Consilia (Helena Quinn, Charlestown, Co Mayo) from Healdsburg moved to Colma to become Superior there. In 1962, the Institute celebrated its Tercentenary, and some of the Sisters travelled to Paris for the celebrations. Following her First Profession, Sr St Oliver arrived back to Colma in August to a warm welcome, and Sr St Maria Assumpta (Carmel O'Sullivan, Co Limerick) arrived from Healdsburg to teach at St Veronica's. August also saw the Sisters learning the results of the General Chapter, which included that 'Saint' was to be dropped from the Sisters' names. In September 1962, Barbara Balbi, who had been in the first graduating class from Holy Angels, became the first Holy Angels past pupil to enter the Institute, and she went to the Drishane Novitiate. She took the name Sr Francis of Assisi. Two further past pupils entered shortly after: Dianne Passalaqua from Healdsburg in 1965, and Patricia Armato, whose family was from St Veronica's Parish, and whose younger sisters had attended St Veronica's school, in 1967.

In the spirit of expansion, the parish began a building fund towards a convent for St Veronica's; donations began to come in from supportive local families, and by 1963 the convent was completed. Many of the Sisters continued their studies, and B.A. degrees were awarded by the University of San Francisco to Sr Attracta, Sr Henry, Sr Louise, Sr Maria Assumpta, Sr Beatrice and Sr Kieran (Mary Nolan, Farranstock, Liselton, Co. Kerry). Late November 1963 brought the shocking news that President Kennedy had been assassinated, recorded in the Annals:

> President John Fitzgerald Kennedy was assassinated in Dallas, Texas. The nation is shocked and stunned by the tragedy. Former Presidents and political leaders of both parties laid aside all other considerations to lead the nation in mourning. Television and radio stations broadcast

---

[55] IJAD, 9th April 1960, *Colma Mission Annals.*
[56] IJAD, 9th November 1960, *Colma Mission Annals.*
[57] IJAD, 20th January 1961, *Colma Mission Annals.*

the sad news to the world... it is hoped that the President will not have died in vain, that his death will awaken the national conscience and form a bond amongst all Americans that will strengthen the nation for good...[58]

By 1965, newspapers in California were reporting the great success of the Institute which had grown in number with twenty-three Sisters working at the three schools including past pupil Sr Francis Balbi who had returned from Drishane to teach at Holy Angels. Sr Francis would become Superior of St Veronica's convent in 1973. One Irish Sister who experienced life at all of the USA convents during the 1960s and 1970s was Sr Pauline O'Dwyer. She arrived in St Veronica's in 1964, moving to Holy Angels in 1966, and then to Healdsburg in 1970 as Superior. In 1972, she became Superior and Principal of Holy Angels school, and Vice Provincial. She recalls that there was always a great spirit in the schools, with emphasis on 'supporting the weaker pupils in order to give them a good start in life.' When a State assessment of schools was introduced between 1975 and 1976, the work done by the Sisters was commended and the schools were found to be excellent.

There were changes in education, in society, and within the Catholic Church from the 1960s onwards that were to have an effect on the role and work of the Sisters in education in the USA. The change was welcomed by the Sisters, who recognised that the increased involvement of lay teachers in schools was necessary. At St Veronica's, a lay Principal was appointed in the late 1970s. By the 1980s, the Sisters had reviewed their presence in California, and decided to place the schools in the hands of lay management. A lay Principal was in place well before the Sisters withdrew from Healdsburg, and indeed the Sisters were pleased to see that many of the teachers appointed at Holy Angels were their own past pupils. At Colma, Sr Helen was Principal until 1987 at which time the parish priest arranged for a group of Franciscan Sisters to take over the school, and the Infant Jesus Sisters left California shortly thereafter. These schools continue to operate, and have maintained their strong academic traditions.

San Francisco, 1950s and 1960s.
L to R: Sr Elizabeth Golden, Sr Rosario McAuliffe
and Sr Pauline O'Dwyer.

---

[58] IJAD, Mother General Rosario, 30th May 1975, in *Naranga Annals*.

THE INFANT JESUS SISTERS IN AUSTRALIA

In 1969, the Archbishop of Melbourne asked the Infant Jesus Sisters to take over the management of St Timothy's School, Forest Hill, in the Vermont suburb of Melbourne. Among the founding members in Vermont were Sr Vincent (Mary McSweeney, Crookstown, Co. Cork), Sr Helen (Hennessy, Castlemartyr, Co. Cork), Sr Henry Golden, Sr Agnes O'Connor, and Mother Pauline Legrix. Sr Henry and Sr Agnes flew to Australia from Ireland, *via* Weybridge. Sr Vincent, Sr Helen and Mother Pauline came to Australia from Malaysia, and their journey from Singapore is recorded in the Annals: they were accompanied to the airport by Mother John Desmond and Mother Damien Murphy and some representatives from Johore Bahru convent and Bukit Timah convent were among the well-wishers there to wave them off. The Sisters marvelled at the seemingly endless hours flying over Australian desert, until they finally landed in Sydney early on Sunday, 19th January. They were welcomed by the Archbishop's secretary, Fr Rebeschini, who drove them to Melbourne. As the new convent building was not yet ready for the Sisters, they were to live temporarily with the Josephite Sisters at their convent in East Hawthorn where on their arrival Revered Fr Brophy, PP, and representatives of Forest Hill parishioners welcomed them.

The area had a youthful population of families with young children, and the school grew quickly. In due course, some of the Sisters also taught at the regional Catholic Secondary school. Over the next few years, additional Sisters arrived to expand the Community. Sr Fidelis O'Connell, Sr Elizabeth (McWey, Kildare Town), Sr Hannah Murray, Sr Vincent McSweeney, and Sr Gertrude (Gertie Lalor, Athy, Co. Kildare), were among those to go to Australia in the late 1960s and early 1970s.

The work of the Sisters expanded in 1972, when they set up another Community and opened a hostel for students in Chadstone, another suburb of Melbourne. The hostel catered for girls from rural districts in Australia, and from the Infant Jesus schools in Malaysia and Singapore, who had come to study in universities and colleges in Melbourne. The opening of this second Australian Foundation was recorded in the Annals: Sr John Desmond came from Penang, Sr Declan (Eileen McSweeney, Crookstown, Co. Cork) came from Teluk Anson, and Sr Fabian Butler from Alor Star. They flew from Singapore, arriving in Melbourne on 17th April 1972, and were welcomed by Sr Gertie and Sr Henry. Throughout the rest of the month of April, the Sisters watched as their new hostel was completed. In May, the two Australian Communities united to welcome the Superior General, Mother Maria del Rosario Brandoly, accompanied by Mother Francis Xavier O'Shea on her first visit to Australia. Mother Rosario attended the inaugural Mass at Chadstone. She later wrote to the Chadstone Community:

> My lighting of the sanctuary lamp for the first time in our little chapel was symbolic of my prayers for the new fraternity: may the flame of their charity radiate in and around the hostel, so that it may be a haven of peace and inspiration for the young girls, who will be welcomed here, and a witness of fraternal love to all.

Late in May 1972, the hostel was ready for habitation, and Sr Fabian and Sr Hannah moved in to get the rooms ready. By June, the first students had arrived: Sophie Chang from Ipoh, Yvonne Lee from Singapore, and an Australian girl, Joy Paterson. In addition, some Sisters who were studying also lived at the hostel. There was discussion about a name for the building, and finally the Sisters settled on 'Naranga', an Aboriginal word meaning 'open and welcoming'. Recalling her years at Naranga, Sr Fabian commented on how the Sisters tried to ensure that the hostel felt like a home to the students and that the atmosphere was relaxing. 'We had no rules', Sr Fabian noted. 'We said to the girls, you make your own rules.' When the girls brought their supper with them to watch TV, Sr Fabian gently suggested that it might be nicer to have meals together at the table. The students seemed happy with that suggestion and enjoyed dining with the Sisters; they even went so far as to invite Sr Fabian to go to the pub with them one evening. 'So I did', Sr Fabian continued. 'They were dancing and singing, very little drinking at that time... it was very interesting'. The students felt sufficiently at home with the Sisters that one student, Chong Wai, had her twenty-first birthday party at the hostel, 'since it was her home'.[59]

The hostel continued to attract new students, and by February of 1974 it was full and the Sisters were turning away applicants for places. There was discussion about the need to extend the building. In the summer of 1974, work started at Naranga to create a new wing and it was partly ready for occupancy by February 1975. That year, Mother General arrived in Australia for her second visit. The two Australian communities came together at Chadstone from 17th to 25th May, and then moved to Vermont until Mother Rosario's departure on 30th May. Mother General's visit allowed time for several discussions on the Sisters' religious life, recorded by Mother General in the Annals:

> The main emphases were on Community and Mission: a development really of No. 18 Book of the Institute. 'Our faithfulness to Christ present in His people demands of us a constant effort to know and understand people in and through the cultural and social environment that is proper to them ... we shall frequently reflect on the value and effectiveness of our apostolic methods; in this way, every possible means will be taken to advance the spread of the Gospel.' It could mean that, as time goes on, more urgent needs may become possible for us to fulfil and if they do, they would find us available.[60]

Early in 1976, some of these needs became evident to the Sisters as they reviewed their apostolic activity. In February 1976, it is recorded that the Sisters, reflecting on their apostolic mission, became interested in 'an appeal made by Bishop Jobst, who was Bishop of the Diocese of Broome.'[61] He was looking for two teachers for a small school, similar to many bush schools, which catered for about fifty-five Aboriginal children. Sr Hannah was interested in responding to the request and promised the Bishop that she would put the project before the General Council, in Rome in March.

When Sr Hannah was en route to Rome, she had the opportunity to stop at the Beagle Bay Mission, an area comprising 700,000 acres of bush where there had been missionaries for almost eighty years. She became convinced of the need for the Institute to work with clergy and other congregations in Beagle Bay, to provide teaching and training for Aboriginal people. In the Autumn of 1976, Sr Hannah went to Sydney to commence a course of studies on the Aboriginal way of life and culture, together with Sr Brid de Courcy MacDonnell, who had come from Ireland. In February 1977, the two Sisters started their mission in Beagle

[59] IJAD, 15th June 1974, *Naranga Annals.*
[60] IJAD, Mother General Rosario, 30th May 1975, in *Naranga Annals.*
[61] IJAD, February 1976, *Naranga Annals.*

Bay. Writing to the Sisters, the Bishop of Broome said: 'Beagle Bay is in the difficult phase of passing management and ownership to the people themselves. You, Sisters, will play an important part in helping the Aborigenes at this junction ... it is no easy mission.'[62]

In April of 1978, two members of the General Council, Sr Valerie Tseng and Sr Raphael Moore, visited Australia spending time with each of the three Communities and reflecting on the Australian mission. The Communities considered that the time was coming to concentrate their efforts on their work with the Aboriginal people. The Sisters recorded that 'spiritually and humanly [Aboriginal] people were at their lowest...' and there were 'too many government and other advisors for a people unable to cope with the complex administration of white Australia.'[63] The Sisters decided to withdraw from Vermont and Chadstone, and found a house in Perth, closer to Beagle Bay. In 1980 they took a private house in Lockridge where they would remain until 1989 The move to Perth records that, on 5th February, 'Sr Fabian Butler and Sr Mary O'Connell left to put the kettle on at Lockeridge'. Two days later, Sr Gertie Lalor and Sr John Desmond joined them. It was an area of state housing and blocks of flats where many low-income families lived in crisis situations. The Sisters found that women were particularly afflicted with suffering, from poverty and abuse, and many were 'just at survival level.' The Sisters wrote: 'It is among these distressed people that some of us found our new apostolate'.[64] Of this move from Melbourne to Perth, Sr Raphael signed the Annals with the words:

> We were most impressed by the Spirit of faith, simplicity and abandonment to Providence which was lived out by all the Sisters and which is characteristic of our Congregation. We are convinced that the sacrifices made by the Sisters in uprooting themselves from a people they loved, will blossom forth into new life in Perth and bear abundant fruit. Moving into the unknown is not easy but surely the loving Father who has brought us this far will continue to be faithful – nothing is impossible for God.[65]

[62] IJAD, Australian Mission Collection. Typescript 1977.
[63] IJAD, Australian Mission Collection. Typescript, 'Our Australian Mission', c 1978.
[64] IJAD, 10th February 1980, *Australia Annals.*
[65] IJAD, Sr Raphael Moore, General Councillor, 5th December 1979, in *Australia Annals.*

Sr Gertie Lalor in Australia

Drishane, waving the train in the 1950s.

Changing

CONTENTS

THE SECOND VATICAN COUNCIL

I J RELIGIOUS LIFE AFTER THE SECOND VATICAN COUNCIL

When Pope John XXIII was elected in October 1958, his was widely perceived as a 'caretaker' appointment, an interim arrangement to allow some breathing space after the long reign of Pius XII. He was an unknown and, already 77 years of age, was not expected to achieve very much during what would undoubtedly be a short reign. Very soon after taking up office, he announced his intention to convene what was always referred to then as an Oecumenical Council. The whole Church was united in prayer for the success of this initiative from the moment of its announcement. The Drishane family, Sisters and pupils, engaged very closely with the preparations for the Council. They began a novena on the 26th September 1962 and listened to Radio Éireann which relayed pontifical High Mass from Vatican Radio on the 11th October 1962, the day the Council was officially declared open. Sadly, Pope John XXIII died the following June, by which time Drishane was equipped with a television set installed in the recreation hall where all followed the prayers and final obsequies broadcast from St Peter's in Rome.

Pope John XXIII was succeeded by Pope Paul VI and the Council continued through its second session. To mark the opening of the third session on September 4th 1964, the Annals note that Pope Paul VI offered the first concelebrated Mass with twenty-four Council Fathers from various nations. The liturgical changes being decreed by the Council were already being put into effect. The introduction of the vernacular Mass was noted on Sunday March 7th 1965 and the fact that for the first time, on June 7th 1965, Mass was said in Drishane with the priest facing the people. The missionary Sisters, in particular, were delighted with these developments which made so much sense in countries whose culture and language did not easily relate to Latin. The Sisters at home were overjoyed to have Mass in English in Drishane and in Irish when they went on holiday to Ballyferriter.

DECREE ON THE ADAPTATION AND RENEWAL OF RELIGIOUS LIFE

The changes in the liturgy affected the Sisters as members of the universal church. However, one decree affected them in particular as members of a religious order. The Decree on the Adaptation and Renewal of Religious Life, *Perfectae Caritatis*, was proclaimed by Pope Paul VI on October 28th 1965; the *motu proprio*[1], *Ecclesiae Sanctae,* was issued on August 6th 1966. It is not an exaggeration to say that the implementation of this decree changed the lives of the Sisters for ever. The document required each congregation to hold a special general chapter within two years. The Infant Jesus Sisters had theirs in Rome in 1968, the main purpose of which was to revise the constitutions. This was a major piece of work which required them to go back to their roots, to learn through reading and prayer the original intention of their founder Père Nicolas Barré (1621-1686), in order to gain a deep knowledge of their original spirit, so that they could bring about genuine renewal. The Acts of that extraordinary General Chapter were distributed to all the communities throughout

---

[1] Administrative papal document which sets out how the decree must be put into practice.

the world, and it was up to each Province to interpret and implement them. Some points were left for decision at Provincial level.

Mother St Gabriel (Elizabeth Browne, Firies, Co. Kerry) resigned on health grounds in 1968 and was succeeded as Provincial Superior by Mother St Philip (Sr Catherine Golden, Cork City). She then became the key person in the Province responsible for seeing that the spirit of Vatican II was understood and implemented in their lives by the Sisters in the province of England and Ireland. Forty years later it is hard to grasp the changes that were required in almost every aspect of religious life at that time, and to appreciate the depth and breadth of them.

PERSONAL RESPONSIBILITY

Perhaps the most significant change was the emphasis placed on personal responsibility. Obedience had always been one of the three vows taken by religious and, over the years – indeed, the centuries – had come to be interpreted in a very narrow way. The voice of the Superior was the voice of God for a religious. There was no discussion after an 'obedience' had been given, and certainly no consultation beforehand. The very mind-set of the religious sisters needed to be changed. The essence of the new thinking was a complicating factor for the Provincial Superior: to impose it would be to contravene it. It required of the Sisters close reading of the Council documents; education in the new way of thinking through attending courses given by the theologians and scholars of the day; discussion in community groups. The impact of the change was different for different Sisters; some relished the new approach to Obedience:

> Oh! I always said it: I never began to live until after [Vatican II]. First time I began
> to live. You know, you were no longer boxed in. You had a mind of your own.
> That is really true. I always said it and will always say it. The freedom![2]

Others found it daunting – they missed the certainty which the older dispensation provided, and resisted the processes which the new one required. Few of the Sisters fell entirely into one or other of those categories; most of them struggled with some elements and welcomed others. Already in her letter to the communities in September 1968, Sr Catherine was encouraging them to embrace the new freedom:

> Freedom is a wonderful thing. The fact that people abuse freedom is not a reason
> for depriving everyone of freedom. Religious life is something we have deliberately chosen.
> Why? To give ourselves to God? In order to work better for His Glory? To ensure
> our own salvation? To help save souls? Whatever our motive was, we now have a chance
> at every moment of the day to deliberately choose His Will again[3]

It was Sr Catherine's responsibility to help the Sisters to interpret the concept of Freedom in a practical way as it applied to them in their daily activities. One example of this is their use of money:

> Formerly a Superior might be considered mean if she mentioned financial considerations

---

[2] Sr Martha Hickey, interview with the authors, July 2008.
[3] IJAD, Provincial letter, 26th September 1968.

to the Sisters. Nowadays it is firmly established that all funds are Community property and the Superior has the obligation of regulating them responsibly.[4]

GOING HOME

One of the more practical expressions of the Second Vatican Council in the lives of the Sisters was the liberalisation of home visits. Before the Second Vatican Council, they went home only before they went out to the Missions; and they went to the Missions for life. Fortunately, many of them came back to Ireland for various reasons, whether for further study or to take up a post elsewhere. One of the big changes brought about by the Council was that they would now come home regularly, and the Sisters living and working in Ireland and England would go home to their families every year.

> You see, the Vatican Council changed everything... now the regular thing is three years. But my mother – they allowed me to come home to see her every year. Wasn't that great? One of the priests [in Japan] said, 'That's humane ...' My mother used to say, 'I can't go to heaven; I have to give you the chance to come home every year.' So she lasted to 102![5]

CONSULTATION

Throughout this time, the new ways of thinking and of 'being' in community were being worked out in group meetings. The Provincial Superior was trying to ensure that the Sisters learned what the Vatican Council had said and how it related to them. Two important meetings were held in Rosslyn House in Weybridge, the aim of which was to show them that there were other ways of being an IJ Sister and other places to be besides Drishane. Various speakers came along – Anton Wallich-Clifford, the founder of the Simon Community, for instance – in order to demonstrate new ways of serving:

> We developed a wider interpretation of the word 'education'. That was terribly important because education had come to be understood for us in the narrow sense of the school classroom. Because - if we go back to our roots - we weren't meant to be cloistered, in the way that we could be in Drishane.[6]

GENERAL CHAPTER 1971[7]

When the 'regular' General Chapter met in 1971, it was the conclusion to a long programme of work, spread over the previous four years. This work had been undertaken in all the Provinces of the Institute and was genuinely consultative. However, only a General Chapter could give effect to the findings. The Acts of the General Chapter 1971 are divided into four sections: Daily Life; Government; Formation; Various Questions. The Chapter looked at adaptation and changes in the work undertaken by the Sisters and concluded that every work which contributed to the formation of the human person towards Salvation was education in the Faith. It urged that creativity should not be the prerogative of new works. The Sisters would continue to be involved in teaching. However, in view of the possible

---

[4] IJAD, Provincial letter, Feast of Our Lady of Lourdes, 1969.
[5] Sr Clare O'Callaghan, interview with the authors, July 2008.
[6] Sr Catherine Golden, interview with the authors, July 2008.
[7] IJAD, Acts of the General Chapter 1971.

take-over of religious schools by the State, they should be prepared to teach in government schools. It also gave great scope and promise of support and encouragement to those who sensed needs more easily and were daringly creative. The main priority in this regard was to welcome the poor as Christ would welcome them.

NEW DEPARTURES

Change began to happen very quickly. Perhaps the most visible change was that the movement out from Drishane did not take the form of founding a new house but of relocating to where a new apostolate could be undertaken. Some of these new apostolates were established by other religious orders or in conjunction with them, and they came about because of an express invitation from another order. In other cases, an individual Sister felt the call to a certain type of work and took a leap of faith in terms of whether it would be 'successful' or not. Each was working out her own vocation as her own personal responsibility to a far greater extent than would have been possible before the Second Vatican Council.

UPTON 1972

The start of the Sisters' involvement in Upton can be credited to Sr Leonie (Renée Redmond, Fermoy, Co. Cork) who happened to meet Fr Con Cottrell when visiting her friend, Fr Forsyth. Fr Cottrell told her about the Rosminian Fathers' plans to take on the care of adult men with special needs in Upton, Co. Cork. He suggested that she should ask her Superior if perhaps some IJ Sisters might join the Rosminians in this work.[8] Sr Catherine Golden started to plan who would be the best Sisters to take up this new challenge:

> So, I was one of the people chosen, together with Sr Gemma (Marian O'Dwyer, Pallasgreen, Co. Limerick), Sr Ita (Mary Angela Carroll, Bruree, Co. Limerick) and Sr Aloysius (Sheila Duggan, Rockchapel, Co. Cork)...and we were to go and gain some knowledge of the work we were going to do. I spent one year in Liverpool, going out with a social worker... I went on to Woking, for occupational therapy... I was very keen on all different kinds of crafts, so I went to London and spent two and a half years there. I came back prepared for Upton.[9]

It is a sign of the success of Sr Attracta's endeavours that 'the lads' as they were always called were trained to the point where they produced soft toys, rugs and sweaters which went on sale in the little craft shop and at the Upton Steam Rally. The aim of the craft shop was not primarily to make money but to make 'the lads' proud of their achievements and to give them a sense of dignity and self-respect.

Soon the original four Sisters were joined by Sr Lelia (Eileen Sheehan, Bruff, Co. Limerick), Sr Danielle Horgan, Sr Michael (Mary O'Connor, Doneraile, Co. Cork) and Sr Emilie (Mary Nagle, Rathmore, Co. Kerry). Throughout the rest of the 1970s in particular, and even into the 1980s and 1990s, missionaries with many decades of experience in Malaysia,

[8] IJAD, Upton box.
[9] Sr Attracta Gilmore, interview with the authors, July 2008.

Singapore, Japan, America and Australia joined the community in Upton. They brought a great deal to the enterprise, but they all insist on how much 'the lads' brought to them. Sr Agatha had spent almost thirty years in Yokohama teaching small children and she describes the different experience she had in Upton, working with a small group in what was called Social Training, and with individuals in a literacy scheme:

> It is very important not to let myself become frustrated, not to expect results, but to learn to 'waste' time, to listen and try to understand what a lad is 'saying' to me. Once he feels that I care and that he is respected and loved, then a great relationship of mutual trust builds up and he and I feel great! Working with [the lads] has taught me that self-importance, success etc. do not count. Rather, a true love based on the recognition of the dignity and worth of each person who is God's creation, enriches both the giver and the receiver.[10]

The value of the contribution of the IJ Sisters to St Patrick's in Upton was summed up by the Rector:

> The IJs ... hold a very special place in the hearts of the residents who have come to love and revere them. The Sisters are the lads' friends and companions and, since they are always about, they provide continuity and stability and this, along with their special feminine touch, makes Upton a homely and warm place. Their apostolate embraces the lads' parents and families also ... they like to meet the Sisters and they appreciate and value their interest and concern about their own welfare as well as their sons'.[11]

MYROSS WOOD 1973

> We have been approached by the Sacred Heart priests, who run a Retreat House in West Cork, for help in staffing their work. Our immediate reaction could be that we have our own staffing problems. However, two Sisters have expressed an interest in working there at least for a year. The priests are building separate quarters for the Sisters, and are very sincere in their plan that their work needs nuns. The running of such a house gives scope for many talents.[12]

Another opportunity had presented itself to broaden the scope of activity in Ireland, and so two sisters, Sr Adelaide (Ellen O'Sullivan, Knocknagree, Co. Cork) and Sr Réidín (Sheila Scannell, Rathcormac, Co.Cork) set out for Skibbereen. Myross Wood was a retreat centre run by the Missionaries of the Sacred Heart, priests and brothers. This was a new venture for them also. In those years, in the aftermath of Vatican II, there was great demand for courses and seminars for religious renewal, both for members of religious orders and for lay people. The centre was very busy: Sr Adelaide took charge of the catering for the resident Community and for retreatants; Sr Réidín took over the household management and administration. Soon they were joined by Sr Nora (Hartnett, Kanturk, Co. Cork) who spent a year helping with the school retreats and also with catechetical work in the Mercy Convent in Rosscarbery. The Sacred Heart Missionaries held their provincial chapters and their annual retreat there. Regular groups using the facility included Alcoholics Anonymous for Refuge of Strength weekends three times a year; Drishane and other schools went there for their annual retreats. The experience of living in Myross Wood provided 'wonderful

10 IJAD, Upton box, Sr Agatha, 4th January 1986, typescript.
11 IJAD, Upton box, Fr James Flynn, Rector, 3rd September 1981.
12 IJAD, Provincial Superior letter, 7th February 1973.

opportunities for learning and growing in the spiritual life'[13] because of the participation in discussions of the two communities, as well as visiting lecturers, retreat directors and missionaries home on holidays.

In the 1980s the original Sisters were replaced by Sr Madeleine (Bridget Lucey, Mallow, Co. Cork), Sr Ita (formerly Canice) Higgins, Sr Mary (Carmody, Athlacca, Co. Limerick) and Sr Agnes (Kiely, Tubber, Rathmore, Co. Kerry). In the early 1990s they all moved on to other apostolates. The IJ involvement in Myross Wood ended in 1994, after over twenty years of service.

TONLEGEE ROAD 1977

Tonlegee Road was one of the first small IJ communities in Ireland. A letter sent to the other houses at Christmas 1977 outlines very clearly the apostolates of the seven Sisters there at the time:

> Sr Oliver (Deering, Dunlavin, Milltown, Co. Wicklow), home from Malaysia, is always happy and smiling and her deep spirit of prayer is an inspiration to all of us. Sr Eilish (O'Mahony, Clashafree, Bandon, Co. Cork), who is in charge, manages well both the material and the spiritual. Our nurse, Sr Teresa (O'Connor, Ballybrogan, Clonard, Co. Meath), is well on the way to becoming a full-time public health nurse. This year she is attending a full time course at St Mary's Hospital, Phoenix Park and is sponsored by the Eastern Health Board. Sr Anne (Delia Fitzgerald, Ballylanders, Co. Limerick) gives most of her time to the Catholic Youth Council working for the youth of the Diocese. The CYC is an organisation established to promote and support the development of youth work in the Dublin Diocese. In doing this it becomes involved both with young people and those who work with them. Sr Colman (Jo Cremin, Kanturk, Co. Cork) and Sr Evelyn (Foyle, Tubbercurry, Co. Sligo) are teachers on the staff of the National School in Ayrfield. It was an 8-teacher school when Sr Colman joined the staff. Now there are 16 teachers and eventually it will be a 32-teacher school...

> Sr Antoinette (O'Callaghan, Rathcoole, Mallow, Co. Cork) is with us since the day she was received, September 8th. She is at present attending a Formation Course run by the Irish Missionary Union. She and Sr Eilish travel to Kimmage four mornings a week for this course which is attended by about forty novices from several congregations both male and female.

> Our work in the parish is interesting and varied. We work in close collaboration with our three priests and we try to meet with them regularly to plan and review our work together. Three of us are Ministers of the Eucharist and we distribute Holy Communion at the main Masses on Sundays. We are also involved with the parish choir, organising the readers for Sunday Masses and we run a crèche for little ones while the parents attend Mass. Once a month we have Mass in our house for the people of the area. We invite about eight couples each time – it helps the neighbours to get to know one another and it also gives them an opportunity to meet us in our own setting. We do some visitation especially in times of illness, sorrow or trouble of any kind and also in time of special rejoicing and when preparing parents before a baby's baptism (of frequent occurrence here because of the many young newly-married couples around). Then there is the weekly prayer meeting on Wednesdays and the work and regular meetings with the women of the

[13] IJAD, Myross Wood box, Sr Réidín Scannell, typescript.

> parish and best of all the Christ-like service of the SVP of which two of our Sisters
> are members.
>
> Our own community evenings are on Saturdays when we have Mass in our oratory.
> Since our big day at the beginning of the term in Malahide with Sr Raphael and all
> our Sisters in Dublin, we have been studying our Chapter documents along with the
> Bishops' Pastoral The Work of Justice. Being where we are, on the outskirts of the
> city, we can more easily avail ourselves of lectures, seminars, weekend retreats etc.
> Right now we have Fr Jim Thompson in for this weekend. He is doing a splendid workshop
> with us on community living. To live out the lesson is another thing. We would like
> very much to – but that is not enough. We are looking forward to our meeting in Drishane.
> The very thought of being down there together for a few days adds to the joys of Christmas
> (even though it means work and long sittings).[14]

Sr Pauline O'Dwyer, having spent over twenty years in California, came here in 1991. In addition to her presence in the Parish, she has been doing valuable work of identification and classification in the IJ Archive in Clontarf. Sr Hilary O'Rourke, who was one of the pioneers in California, is also active in the Parish.

HARTSTOWN 1980

Sr Noreen (McGrath, Ballybane, Midleton, Co. Cork) and Sr Louise Roche had been teaching in the Junior School in Malahide and Sr Catherine (Lynch, Churchtown, Mallow, Co. Cork) in the Community School there, when they went as pioneers to Hartstown with Sr Antoinette from Tonlegee Road and Sr Helen (Coleman, Belgooly, Kinsale, Co. Cork). The fact that Sr Antoinette had just been professed the previous year and Sr Helen had just returned from Malaysia after forty-four years there, gives an indication of the age range of the community. They had all responded to the spirit of the Provincial Council which was calling for small communities. This was a small community in a new area:

> We moved in at the same time as the people: just housing, nothing else; both partners
> working; the children were only beginning to be born. It was great really because
> everything started with us and with them together, especially in the parish. When I
> think of it now, we were as involved after school as we were during school. School was
> one job, the other was our presence in the parish.[15]

Sr Noreen got a job in Corduff school and Sr Catherine in Blakestown Community School. 'After Malahide it was a new experience for us to teach in a disadvantaged area.'[16]

BALLYMUN 1983

Sr Antoinette O'Callaghan, who was living in North Circular Road community and working as a Social Worker with Travellers in Ballymun, felt that something had to be done for them in the area of education. They had to go on a bus every day to Gardiner Street because no other school would take them. Sr Betty Kelleher (formerly Sr Christine) was in Rathgar at

---

[14] IJAD, Tonlegee Road box. Christmas letter 1977.
[15] Sr Noreen McGrath, interview with the authors, December 2008.
[16] Sr Catherine Lynch, interview with the authors, January 2009.

the time. She had many years experience of teaching in the Junior School in Malahide so she started straight away: 'It was a big change and I had to learn a lot, but it doesn't matter where you are, really – the attraction is love for the children.'

Her aim was to have a pre-school for Traveller children. It was a long road. She was very lucky to find the perfect partner for the project, a parishioner Margaret Williams, who worked with her for seventeen years. They would set out together in the morning in the mini-bus and collect the children from an unofficial site. Sr Betty recalls:

> I think the children were great. They'd never been off a site, or the side of the road, and then two strangers come and take them into a flat that they'd never been in... They had great trust in Sr Catherine O'Driscoll (Daughter of Charity) so they trusted us.[17]

In the beginning there was no money, no furniture in the flat – their first 'table' was a door resting on two chairs – and they really had no idea as to how their dream was to be realised. So, a lot of time was spent at meetings with the local authority and in fundraising activities. Meanwhile, the little children were being taught, and the bigger girls were being trained in child-care so that they would be better equipped to look after their own children. The families were being cared for in lots of ways, including visiting them when there was illness and helping out when a member of the family was dying. As the pre-school grew and they got bigger numbers, they persuaded the Principal of the National School in Ballymun to enrol the children, and that put an end to the bus into Gardiner Street school.

The wider IJ family was very supportive. For example, the children in Portmarnock Community School, when Sr Noreen (Vaughan, Kilnamartyra, Macroom, Co. Cork) was on the staff, started coming to visit the project. They also started inviting the Traveller children to a Christmas party in Portmarnock every year. That tradition continues even though there is no IJ Sister in Portmarnock school and no IJ Sister in the Ballymun school. Last year they celebrated twenty-five years there and Sr Betty returned to Ballymun to find that the dream had become a reality. Margaret Williams is still there: there is a beautiful school for the Travellers – St Margaret's Pre-School – a community centre and a new site.

Sr Betty had started the pre-school in a flat in Ballymun in 1983 and was travelling there every day from Rathgar. Meantime, Fr Sean Holloway, a Columban priest, was keen to have Sisters working in the parish. Sr Raphael Moore, as Provincial, put out the call. There was a lot of talk at the time about small communities; there was also a lot of resistance to it and a fear of 'breaking up community life'. There was a strong feeling on the Provincial Council that those in formation should get experience of small communities and new kinds of work. Sr Eilish O'Mahony was in charge of formation at the time, so she went to Ballymun, as did Sr Betty and Sr Catherine Lynch:

> It was a total shock. It wasn't that I decided to get out of teaching – I enjoyed teaching very much – I had a sense of moving back to the original idea of Père Barré. But then the question arose: what would I do?[18]

Sr Catherine has spent the twenty-three years since then working out the answer to that question, through parish activity, working with groups, and helping people individually – women, and some men – to cope with their lives. 'Women carry the brunt of life here,

17 Sr Betty Kelleher, interview with the authors, January 2009.
18 St Catherine Lynch, interview with the authors, January 2009.

the responsibility for children. They carry the community. They need support and I'll do anything that I can to support them.'

Meanwhile, in the 1970s, Malen del Valle Garcia from Puerto Rico was studying in Spain. She had just attended her first course – as a lay person – on the documents of the Second Vatican Council. It opened her eyes to what her role as a Christian was to be:

> I had - not to *do* it, but - to help people to do it, to help people to realise that they were the Church, that they were the people of God. It wasn't me, *doing*, it was accompanying, being with the people.[19]

By a sequence of events which others might call coincidence – but Sr Malen would call Providence – she had found herself going to university in Spain, instead of in the United States, and staying in a hostel run by the Infant Jesus Sisters, instead of the Sacred Heart Sisters with whom she was educated in Puerto Rico. She joined the congregation in Spain. When she was offered France or Ireland for a year of her novitiate she chose Drishane. She was to return there later to prepare for her Final Profession.

When Sr Malen arrived in Ballymun in 1992, she had been living for two years in Oakfield, Liverpool, developing a retreat team – there were four girls living with the IJ Sisters there and four boys living with the Christian Brothers. When the Oakfield house closed, an opportunity arose to do the same in Ballymun. Because there was no house, the young people were invited to commit themselves for nine months but to live in their own homes. The project started with seven young people. Sr Malen's aim was to train them for leadership. Monday was training day; the trainers were professionals and the participants learned to prepare their own materials. They gave retreats all over the country. The income from this activity was very small, because they were regarded as students. However, Sr Malen managed to have them recognised as volunteers, which meant they could claim the dole. 'It took me ages to get that, but we got it. They were being trained and they had their money.'

Then a greater need arose which required a shift of resources. The Principal in the school was finding that, despite all his best efforts, he had a persistent problem of non-attendance. He called Sr Malen, 'They're hungry. They're not sleeping. What can we do for them without stigmatizing them?' Sr Malen said she would think about it – and so the Ashling Project was born:

> It was for children at risk, 8-12 years of age. They needed a safe place and, at the same time, some structure in their lives. It was a lot of work, but it's eleven years now and we have four centres in Ballymun.[20]

The four centres serve the four areas of Ballymun, in order to be near the schools which the children attend. There is one co-ordinator and two part-timers as well as volunteers. They provide a home-type environment but it is non-residential. They have a dining-room and serve a hot meal. The children are selected for the programme using four criteria and also teacher recommendation. When the group is formed, they are given a few weeks to

---

[19] Sr Malen, interview with the authors, December 2008.
[20] Ibid.

settle into school, and the programme starts at the end of September. It is very much an IJ apostolate, inspired by the writings of Père Nicolas Barré.

Sr Malen has now developed the project further. Realising that the children have even greater difficulty adjusting to the post-primary environment, she began to feel that she should not abandon them after 6th class. So, just this year, she has initiated a support system for those in their first year of post-primary education.

The third Sister in Ballymun is Sr Ann Marie (Ryan, Kilquade, Co. Wicklow) who came from Wolverhampton in 2006. She is busy with parish work, particularly music in the liturgy, as well as keeping elderly people active through exercise and other programmes.

DERRY 1994

Through an intricate web of IJ past pupils and former colleagues, and the encouragement of Sr Mairéad O'Sullivan (Clonkeen, Killarney, Co Kerry) who was Provincial Superior at the time, Sr Mary de Courcy MacDonnell (Athy, Co Kildare) found herself in Derry in 1994:

> At that time [Creggan Community Enterprise] were organising a major conference to highlight the need for services for sexually abused children on the Creggan Estate. It was this group who said that I needed to set up an Art Therapy Service.[21]

Sr Mary found some outstanding art therapists practising under different titles: Probation Officer, Community Artist, Care Worker etc. These had formed NIGAT (Northern Ireland Group for Art as Therapy); she joined them and was generously supported by them. Make Your Mark was formed in 1996 in response to a clear need which she identified. It was through her experience in community development and her commitment to serving the needs of children that the programme came into being. Sr Mary retired in 2000 leaving a service in place with a full-time and two part-time art therapists (all trained and State Registered), two part-time administrators and a full-time development officer. She continues her art therapy in Burton-on-Trent.

BELFAST 2001

Just around that time, Sr Catherine (O'Sullivan, Rathmore, Co. Kerry), after eleven years in Peru, joined the Cornerstone Community in Belfast. A prayer group of people from the four main Christian traditions (Church of Ireland, Methodist, Presbyterian and Roman Catholic) had been formed in 1978, when the 'Troubles' were at their worst and the people were living in fear. It was from this prayer group that Cornerstone Residential Community of three members evolved in 1982. By 2001, when Sr Catherine was one of the three residents, there were sixteen members in the community, both men and women dedicated to peace:

> The symbolic value of being together as an inter-church community in the midst of

---

21 IJAD, Sr Mary de Courcy MacDonnell, *Six Years in Derry*, typescript, 5th October 2008.

> deprivation and polarization, as a SIGN OF HOPE, is the community's most important
> mission... Our house offers hospitality to all who come... We try to preserve a peace and
> calm in the house so that visitors and community members can enjoy quiet moments of
> relaxation, interchange and prayer. The little garden too is an oasis for nourishment, healing
> and communing with the Divine. During the first three months of this year (2001) 390
> people were welcomed to our community... They return to their own countries with
> a new appreciation of the resilience of the local people.[22]

DROMCOLLOGHER 1995

> The sun shone on Dromcollogher, giving extra edge to the sense of celebration and
> pride that washed over the crowd who gathered to greet President Robinson when she
> arrived to open the day care centre and social housing scheme in the village on Thursday.[23]

Sr Fidelma (Frances Hogan, Rathcannon, Kilmallock, Co Limerick), Sr Rosario McAuliffe
and Sr Joan (Scannell, Rathcormac, Co. Cork) who had all gone on their first mission – to
Malaysia and America – in the 1950s, had arrived in Dromcollogher almost a year earlier.
Sr Mairéad O'Sullivan, Provincial Superior stressed, at the welcoming ceremony, that the
important thing for them was that the invitation had come from the local community.
They saw their work as being a presence among the elderly, and they had received an
exceptionally warm welcome from both people and clergy. 'It is right that you would
respect and honour and in every way support older citizens', President Robinson told the
crowd at the official opening. She referred to the co-operative spirit of the area which had
found its expression in the founding of the country's first co-operative creamery in 1889,
and expressed her admiration for Horace Plunkett and those involved in the co-operative
movement. In their time, she went on, they were the forward thinking people, the leaders
and visionaries whose work had left a legacy for future generations, just as what was now
being achieved would also be so important for the future.

OVERSEAS

CAMEROON 1980

In other parts of the Institute also the IJ Sisters were responding to calls for help from new
missions. A concerted effort was made to have an Institute-wide response to these calls
where at all possible. In 1968, a group of five Sisters, from France, Spain and Italy, travelled
to Cameroon in West Africa. In 1975, at the invitation of the Archbishop of Yaoundé, they
went to Saa where they founded CRAT (Centre Rural Appui Technique), a centre of rural
support with the aim of forming local people into leaders in their own villages. It was in
1980 that an Irish Sister, Sr Georgina Clarson (Broadford, Co. Limerick), joined four Sisters
(two Cameroonian, one French, one Italian) and a young Italian lay volunteer there. The
leadership training which they gave covered areas such as hygiene, housekeeping, cooking,
sanitation, first aid, literacy. In addition, training was also given in spiritual leadership. In
a country where the Catholic population is so widely dispersed, the priest cannot say Mass
everywhere every week, so there is a need for lay people to lead prayer services. The aim of
the centre is to help the people to help themselves:

---

[22] IJAD, Sr Catherine O'Sullivan, typescript, May 2001.
[23] IJAD, *Limerick Leader*, Saturday October 26th 1996.

Our greatest enemy is not the heat or the roads but discouragement. There are
so many frustrations even on a material level but we need infinite patience.[24]

The official language is that of the former coloniser, France, and Sr Georgina set about
learning the most widely spoken Cameroonian language of the area, Ewondo. She
expressed delight in her letters when her greetings were understood, and when she began
to be able to follow the sermon at Mass. She also was involved, with the other European
sisters in the country, in efforts to understand the culture and recognise its richness. This
was very much part of the post-Vatican II understanding of missionary activity, with its
stress on inculturation, on the importance of getting into the rhythm of the country, into
the realisation that African attitudes can be very different from European ones. The Sisters
have to be particularly sensitive to cultural differences when young Cameroonian women
express an interest in the religious life. The first Cameroonian IJ, Sr Brigitte (Ongbilip),
made her final vows in 1980. Later that year she moved out with a group of sisters to set
up a separate community – the first African IJ community and also the first all-African
community in the diocese – in order to develop an African style of religious life.[25]

A major part of the work of the Sisters everywhere is 'being with' the people. They go
wherever the people are and respond to whatever their needs are. In Cameroon, rather than
bringing the people into a centre, the Sisters went out to the villages. They would send word
to a certain village that on such and such a day they would be there. Then it was up to one of
the village leaders to gather the people together. Work was done out in the open air, under a
tree or near someone's house. The people assembled from 9 am, singing and dancing and
creating a good atmosphere. Then, instruction of the women in needlework, or hygiene,
went on all day at a leisurely pace. Over time these visits developed into important social
occasions for the men and the children as well.

By the end of her first year, Sr Georgina was teaching three days a week in the secondary
school.[26] It meant that she could not go to work in the villages very much, but it helped her
to have more contact with the young. On the other days her work in CRAT continued. She
helped the catechists who were teaching the children in the villages. These were ordinary
lay people who had not had much training and needed a good deal of help.

Sr Noreen McGrath responded to a request from Cameroon for Sisters in 1986. She was
very interested in the Basic Christian Communities, as she explained:

There were about fourteen communities at the time and there could be twenty, thirty
or forty people in each. They shared the gospel of the Sunday and asked themselves,
how can I apply that to my life this week? I found that very powerful actually. Often
there were rows and arguments and differences, but on the whole they prayed and
reflected together and worked in the parish.[27]

Then there was the work around the dispensary – run by Sr Paul (Jacqueline Lamotte), a
dentist by profession – just being there to encourage the people, to listen to them, and to
face with them whatever they had to face. 'They are extraordinary, a very resilient people.
So little can make them happy.' And now in 2009, forty years after the first European IJ

[24] IJAD, Sr Georgina Clarson, letters from Cameroon.
[25] Sadly, Sr Brigitte died on the 24th April 1998.
[26] IJAD, Cameroon box, Sr Georgina Clarson, 24th November 1980.
[27] Sr Noreen McGrath, interview with the authors, December 2008.

Sisters went out, there are seventeen Cameroonian Sisters. They are running a school for deaf and dumb children; they are running a health clinic; it is now local Sisters working for the local Church: 'But they are keen to have me, so I'm going back – I wouldn't have gone back except for that.'

They are working hard with the women in the villages: they have set up a mill for grinding maize – the staple diet of the people – and people come there to grind their maize from other villages. The idea is to replicate that in another village. The work continues with the women: parenting skills; craftwork; health education particularly Aids education; soap-making; setting up literacy classes. The tradition in the rural areas is for the women to work the fields and have children; they are coming out of that traditional role now and the challenge is to develop their talents and skills.

NIGERIA 1983

In the early 1980s, the Sisters in Cameroon began to talk about investigating a mission in neighbouring Nigeria. It would be an English-speaking mission (which might prove more attractive for Irish sisters). And so, Sr Georgina Clarson with Sr Marguerite Marie Carsana, an Italian Sister based in France, and Sr Ana de Travy from Spain, who had spent many years in Malaysia, including some years as Novice Mistress there, headed out on an excursion to Nigeria in February 1981. Crossing into the south of the country – where they had intended locating but, because of a series of providential incidents, did not – the Sisters remarked on how prosperous it seemed:

> Once in Nigeria we had beautiful roads. It is the first big difference you notice. Nigeria is a richer country.[28]

However, as they continued on the road north, they felt they were travelling further and further away from prosperity into an area more likely to be in need of help.

The following year Nigeria was in the news because of the visit in February of Pope John Paul II. The image painted in the mass media was of a flourishing Nigerian church with seminaries full to overflowing. Nigeria was presented as the richest country in Africa:

> This created doubts in our minds about the advisability of a foundation there. Is this really the place for the Daughters of Père Barré?[29]

The decision was taken that the General Council would visit in June 1982 and that, in advance of that visit, Sr Georgina Clarson and Sr Kathleen Day would carry out a detailed study of the situation over a period of six weeks, in order to have 'sound elements to base our discernment.' Arising out of those visits and that report, it was decided to establish a first community at Jalingo, Taraba State.

The departure for the new mission was planned for the 31st January 1983. However, this was a time of great confusion in the region. Television reports showed a massive exodus of

---

[28] IJAD, Cameroon box, Sr Georgina Clarson, 1st March 1981.
[29] IJAD, Nigeria box, Superior General and General Council, Rome, 25th August 1982.

illegal immigrants from Nigeria, and the situation seemed chaotic. Having been assured that the media were exaggerating, and that everything was functioning normally, the founding Sisters left Rome on the 25th February 1983. Sr Kathleen Day was the only Irish Sister among the pioneers. Before taking up residence in their new house in Jalingo (which was not yet completed), they took an intensive course in Hausa, the principal language of the area.

The Bishop's idea had been that the Sisters would set up schools, but they resisted that for two reasons. In the rest of the Institute, they were coming out of the big schools. Secondly, when Nigeria got its independence the schools that had been run by religious orders were taken over by the State. By March Sr Kathleen was writing:

> Next week, Jenny (IJ Sister from Malaysia) and I hope to start looking for jobs. If we get them, Ana and Gloria (Garcia Innes, Spain) will be able to go full time to the villages and, hopefully, we'll switch around after a while. Primary schools have been closed here now for the past ten months – no salaries for teachers.[30]

This was quite an experience for Sr Kathleen who had come almost straight from being Principal of the Community School in Malahide:

> ... I had not only the forty in the classroom but also on the window ledges, everywhere. You never knew how many you had... and they had no books...After a few years we gave in to the Bishop and agreed that at least we'd start a primary school.[31]

A development grant channelled through the Irish Missionary Resource Service funded the building of the school.

Another important function of the IJ Sisters in Nigeria was to encourage young Nigerian women to join the Congregation. The first issue to be addressed was their education. It was decided that, if they were to join, they should repeat at least the last two years of secondary school, but there was no such school in the area. The Bishop was happy to have the girls attend the Seminary in Yola, as long as one of the Sisters came to teach there. Again, that was not part of their original plan, but of course they accepted it. They started in one of the staff houses on the Seminary grounds and the girls came to live there while they attended school and later teacher training college. About a year later they moved into their own house.

Sr Breda Madigan (Charleville, Co. Cork), back home after more than twenty years in Penang and Singapore, went out to Nigeria in 1987. However, after two years she was elected to serve on the Central Council in Rome which brought to an end her third overseas mission. Sr Anne O'Neill (Ballineen, Co. Cork), who was in Cameroon from 1988, went to Nigeria in 2000. She was joined there by Sr Antoinette O'Callaghan in 2002 and Sr Bernadette O'Reilly (Kells, Co. Meath) in 2003. There are now nine Nigerian Sisters there as well as Sr Maria Jesus Major from Spain and Sr Caterina Dolci from Italy. In October 2008 the Nigerian IJ mission celebrated its Silver Jubilee for which the pioneers returned.

---

30 IJAD, Sr Kathleen Day, 5th March 1983.
31 Sr Kathleen Day, interview with the authors, December 2008.

PERU 1970

> The Central Team asked me if I would go to South America ... I could only see myself in
> Malaysia – I was twenty-seven years there – and I was trying to discern ... and then the
> dreadful news came from Peru: Sr Pat Condon was killed in a car crash. Immediately,
> as if the writing was on the wall, I knew that Peru was for me. It was just as clear as
> crystal that this was my mission.[32]

It was 1986. Sr Pat Condon (formerly Sr St Oliver, California) had been seventeen years in
Peru, mainly in the shanty town of Collique outside Lima. The Peruvian mission had been
founded from Spain and Sr Pat moved there from Healdsburg, California, where she had
been teaching for seven years. Although she never quite mastered the Spanish language,
she communicated very effectively with the people, particularly those with special needs,
because of her faith, her energy and her smile – La Madre Sonrisa, the newspaper heading
for the account of her funeral called her. In a letter to Ireland in the aftermath of her death,
Fr Kevin Gallagher SJ, who worked with Sr Pat in the Fe y Alegria school system, wrote:

> Pat was the incarnation ... of the gospel, of Christ's love and concern for everyone even
> to the most insignificant and the most deformed. [The people's grief at her funeral]
> made me proud to be part of the Church that Pat was a witness to. It also made me
> think a lot about just what is important in life and in our work. Pat was not an intellectual;
> she was not a natural leader, humanly speaking. And she was not really very fluent in
> Spanish. But she had the power of love and concern deep in herself and it just came out
> so many times over so many years that she was a living example of the beatitudes.[33]

In the last year of her life, Sr Pat took a sabbatical back in Ireland-England, but she returned
to Peru, this time to the newly-formed shanty town of Mi Peru in Ventanilla on the other
side of Lima, and wrote home to her Sisters in Ireland:

> I've plunged once again into the mission here in Peru. I thank God every day for your
> part and His in making this possible. What a joy it is to be able to return with good
> health and help start off another project![34]

Seven months later, Sr Pat was dead. The tragedy of her fatal traffic accident on the 3rd
October 1986 proved the catalyst for Sr Catherine's departure for Peru. Having spent some
time in Spain learning the language, she arrived in Collique and found letters from Ireland,
Malaysia, Australia and Africa, all coming together to help her take her first steps in South
America. 'It was great to feel the same spirit of hospitality and openness right across the
world.'[35]

Having arrived late at night, she was dismayed, the following morning in the light of day,
to see the dry hills of sand and rock, without a tree, flower or blade of grass, so different
from the lush vegetation she was used to in Malaysia, but by evening she felt a deep sense
of satisfaction in that she was situated right in the midst of the people. This sense of being
with the people comes through strongly in all the letters from Peru, as well as a conviction
that their 'contribution is like a drop in the ocean and it is the Lord, working through His
people, who has to do the work.' Sr Catherine used to move around, talk to the people, sit
on a stone outside their house – very often a straw sort of hut – and listen to them.

---

[32] Sr Catherine O'Sullivan, interview with the authors, July 2008.
[33] IJAD, Peru box, Fr Kevin Gallagher SJ, 15th October 1986.
[34] IJAD, Peru box, Sr Pat Condon, 10th March [1986].
[35] IJAD, Sr Catherine O'Sullivan, 16th March 1988.

By 1995 she was commenting on the great difference made by having piped water twice a week. More and more patches of green could be seen. Also, there were a lot more public telephones (but no private ones yet). However, the Sisters were committed to supporting the people through education rather than by giving them material things. From time to time people send money, the proceeds of fund-raising, and the Sisters put it towards the cost of a special teacher for a Down's syndrome group, for example. The Sisters don't look for an outcome, a goal achieved, but rather an improvement in the day-to-day lives of the people through providing support for their own creativity and initiative. As Sr Catherine recalled:

> They were wonderful people – I was just in awe of them. They were so cheerful. I learned and I was convinced that there are no difficulties in life after this, only challenges, and that within each challenge there's always something positive. If you can't change the situation, you learn how to cope with the situation. I learned from the people there. They were really wonderful. I was there for eleven years and I just loved being there... they brought out the best in me and I hope that I brought out the best in them... I would love to feel that the people are living their lives as they want to live their lives and that they are able to continue to bring the best out of others.[36]

BOLIVIA 2005

Sr Catherine returned to South America in 2005 and spent a further two years, this time in Bolivia. It was a mining area so the children, from as young as twelve, were working in the mines. The Sisters tried, by providing for their education through scholarships, to keep them out of work for as long as possible in order to improve their lives. The young people who got the scholarships worked for three hours a week with other groups more needy than themselves, for example, in children's homes or in the home for the senior citizens. Or they worked with mining children who were not able to go to school. The Sisters used to bring them together and teach them in the evenings. 'But they never got handouts. They were wonderfully creative.'[37]

CZECH REPUBLIC

Since the year 1998 there has been an IJ presence in the Czech Republic. This new phenomenon arises from the fact that a group of young Czech women, among them Sr Veronika Řeháková from Brno, was attracted by the writings of Nicolas Barré. In 2002, Veronika came to England to experience various ministries and to continue her formation. She made her first commitment in 2005 as a member of the province of England and Ireland. She then decided to return to her native country where she works as a teacher. Sr Georgina Clarson, whose ministry includes teaching English, is with her in Brno.

---

[36] Sr Catherine O'Sullivan, interview with the authors, July 2008.
[37] Ibid.

MALAHIDE CLOSING

NORTH CIRCULAR ROAD 1983

The Provincial Council began reflecting on the future of Malahide during the summer of 1981 and this led to discussion about alternative accommodation for the Sisters. It became clear that another house was needed in Dublin in any case and this gave the opportunity to move out a small group from the Malahide community. The founding Sisters of the North Circular Road house in 1983 were Sr Francis Xavier O'Shea, Sr Eithne (Ellen McCarthy, Tallow, Co. Waterford), Sr Consilia Quinn, Sr Perpetua (Mary O'Brien, Midleton, Co. Cork), Sr Antoinette O'Callaghan and Sr Teresa O'Connor. They were joined in January 1984 by Sr Rita Murphy and the following year by Sr Eileen Sheehan and Sr Eucharia (Catherine O'Callaghan, Banagh, Kanturk, Co. Cork). The apostolates of the various members of the community, as recorded in the Annals, ranged over social work with the Travellers, adult education, pastoral work, home visitation, ministry of Word and Eucharist in the parish church, work with the Saint Vincent de Paul Society and the Legion of Mary, helping in a club for schizophrenics, and hospital visitation. In June 1985 the Annals record Sr Teresa's delight when she got a new appointment in a mobile clinic for Travelling people. By 1989, Sr Perpetua O'Brien was the only surviving founder member of the community; she and Sr Rita Murphy had been joined by Sr Helen Hennessy, Sr Eileen Sheehan, Sr Eilis (Ahern, formerly Sr St Benignus) and Sr Betty. The house was closed in 1998.

PORTMARNOCK 1985

Father Enda Lloyd, who was in Portmarnock when the Sisters were leaving Malahide, was so keen to have them relocate to his parish that he helped to find a suitable house. They moved in on April 10th 1985 and got a warm welcome from priests and people. The pioneers were Sr Etienne Hyland, Sr Mary (O'Sullivan, Killarney, Co. Kerry), Sr Mary Peter (Weedle, Mallow, Co. Cork), Sr Margaret Tarrant, Sr Norrie and Sr Noreen Vaughan. Fr Lloyd advised them to take things slowly. His main wish was that the house should be a house of prayer, of peace, of welcome, an oasis in the parish where people could come to chat, to discuss things, to pray.

Sr Noreen was already teaching fulltime in the nearby Community School and was very involved in the pastoral care programme there.

> I also started Junior SVP because I felt it is important for children to make a contribution to others different from themselves. They worked with the physically and mentally handicapped... They were involved in an ARCH group... It had a huge impact in the lives of the children who went... It increased their sense of their own worth... Two offshoots of that: in some cases it influenced their career choice but also, when they were out, if they came across prejudice, they always opposed it ... I never knew that could happen, but it did.[38]

---

[38] Sr Noreen Vaughan, interview with the authors, January 2009.

Sr Eleanor Nevill moved to Portmarnock in 1987 and worked for some years in the Community School with Sr Noreen. When Sr Noreen retired from teaching, Sr Eleanor thought it was time for her to retire too. However, neither Sister has stopped working. Sr Noreen continued to work with groups in the parish, including preparation for the Sacrament of Confirmation. Her more recent interest is in the environment. She is involved in training people to promote an environmentally sustainable, spiritually fulfilling, socially just, human presence on this planet for our future.

Sr Eleanor embarked on a lifetime of teaching in the Novitiate, when she was asked by her Mistress of Novices to teach French. Having taught in St Maur's in Weybridge during World War II – where she experienced rationing as well as the occasional air-raid 'but no direct hit' – and in Malahide, she moved to Rathgar, and the opportunity arose to teach in the women's prison at Mountjoy. Sr Eleanor recalls:

> I went in on my bicycle every day to the women's prison. I had no problems in the traffic – oh except once, maybe twice, I came off it but it wasn't my fault and the driver wanted to give me a lift but I got back up again and I was fine. It was the time when HIV-AIDS was rampant in the prison, and there was a lot of ignorance about it. I remember they made tea for me and I think they were trying me out to see if I'd drink it from their mug. But I had read all about it and knew I couldn't catch it from them.[39]

Over seventy years after her first attempt at teaching, she teaches adults to read: 'I just think everybody has a right to be able to read, nobody should be denied that right. It's not because I'm an IJ Sister – it's just that!'

211 CLONTARF ROAD 1985

On the longest day of the year 1985, the last Sisters left the Community house in Malahide for their new home in Clontarf. The Annals record: 'It poured cats and dogs, and with hearts breaking and backs aching we left the back door for good.'[40]

On arriving at the very blustery seafront in Clontarf to unpack the removal van, Sr Eilis and Sr Noreen provided meals-on-wheels until they could find their own pots and pans. When all the helpers had gone home, the Sisters just stood in the dusk looking out on the beauty of the bay. They followed the lights and picked out the North Wall, Dun Laoghaire and Howth, but not a trace of Malahide. It was gone from their horizon. At 11 pm they noticed a huge bulk of light moving out slowly from the shore and prayed to God to help all who were leaving home and were lonely on that boat. Sr Emilie cheered them all up by reminding them that they were lucky to be where they were: 'We're home at last.' Sr Brendan (Sheila Scollard, Milltown, Co. Kerry), writing this account, added that if Browning were among them, he would have said:

> Grow old along with me!
> The best is yet to be
> The last of life, for which the first was made,
> Our times are in His hand

---

[39] Sr Eleanor Nevill, interview with the authors, January 2009.
[40] IJAD, 211 Clontarf Road box.

Who saith "a whole I planned,
Youth shows but half, trust God, see all,
Nor be afraid."

The founding Sisters of this house were: Sr Aloysius (Sheila Duggan, Rockchapel, Newmarket, Co. Cork), Sr Flannan (Katie Galvin, Kilnamona, Co. Clare), Sr Emilie, Sr Brendan, Sr Maureen Roddy, Sr Celestine, Sr Joan Scannell, and Sr Catherine (Shanahan, Farranfore, Co. Kerry). Sr Catherine, having spent almost twenty years in Japan, took up a fulltime post in the Holy Faith Convent in Clontarf and taught there until her retirement. They were joined a few years later by Sr Catherine (formerly Senan Fitzgerald, Liscarroll, Co. Cork), Sr Perpetua O'Brien and Sr Monica (Kelly, Shanagolden, Co. Limerick). When the North Circular Road house closed in 1998, Sr Eileen Sheehan came here, and Sr Ann Breen in 2000. When the Weybridge house closed, Sr Carmel O'Sullivan came in 1996. They became active in the parish as Ministers of the Word, Eucharist and Music, as well as in various parish groups such as bereavement support and hospitality to alleviate loneliness.

DRISHANE CLOSING

MILLSTREET

When Drishane closed in 1992, a group of Sisters moved into the town of Millstreet and with great charity and good humour set about forming a community in Drishane House on the Killarney Road. The Annals list the pioneers as Sr Raphael Moore, Sr Vincent (Johanna Mulcahy, Castlelyons, Co. Cork), Sr Mary (Cotter, Doneraile, Co. Cork), Sr Patricia (Maud Collins, Carrowmore, Ballina, Co. Mayo), Sr Benedict (Ellie Cronin, Scartaglen, Castleisland, Co. Kerry), Sr Leonie Redmond, Sr Alphonsus McMahon, Sr Mary Catherine (Marren, Sligo), Sr Aloysius (Eileen O'Driscoll, Ballyheigue, Co. Kerry), Sr Consilia Quinn, Sr Marie Celine (Mary Shortall, Thurles, Co. Tipperary), Sr Colette (Kathleen O'Connor, Strokestown, Co. Roscommon), Sr Helen (Falvey, Milltown, Co. Kerry) and Sr Peter Fahy. The bonds of friendship between Drishane and the town of Millstreet were of such long standing that they simply continued. The apostolate was as various as the Sisters in the house. The first one listed is 'care of each other' and this is characteristic of all the houses, whatever the range of ages. The house welcomed all-comers. People from the town came to prayer meetings during Lent and Advent. Interest in missionary work and the work of the Sisters in other ministries was clear from the correspondence kept up with them and the welcome given to them when they visit. Sr Peter Fahy, who had taught in Drishane for most of her career, travelled from this Community to Cork to continue as a fulltime teacher in Ballincollig Community School until her retirement in 2008.

CORK

St Joseph's, Model Farm Road

The Acts of the General Chapter 1989 were presented to the Sisters of the Province in a series of meetings and reflected upon. The Sisters grappled with new understandings of Evangelisation and Apostolic spirituality. They summed up their insight under the following headings:

What?   Evangelisation is a reciprocal process. We both give and receive.

Why?   The Risen Christ is important to us; that is the message we long to share wherever or however with whom we can.

How?   Above all by BEING. We are called to be free, real authentic witnesses, a presence (Christ's presence).

OPEN   to the Spirit, to the needs of others, to our need to be evangelised.[41]

This is very much the understanding in evidence in St Joseph's which opened its doors to the first three elderly Sisters on November 23rd 1989. They were Sr John Desmond, who had spent over fifty years in Malaysia and, incredibly, a further ten years in Australia; Sr Francis Xavier O'Shea who had spent over thirty years in Malaysia followed by twelve years on the General Council in Paris; and Sr Madeleine Lucey, who first went out to Singapore in 1933.

Sr Carmel (Eileen McMahon, Newcastlewest, Co. Limerick) came here as Superior, having just spent six years as Provincial Superior and six years on the General Council. As it turned out, her time in St Joseph's was to be an interlude between those leadership roles and two terms as Superior General. So, in 1995, a past pupil of Drishane was elected to serve in the highest office in the Institute, the first Irish Sister to do so in almost 333 years of its history.

Sr Carmel, Sr Brendan (Bridget Cronin, Scartaglen, Castleisland, Co. Kerry) and Sr Agnes Kiely, who had been working hard for about a month in advance of the opening, welcomed the first Sisters. That welcome has continued throughout the twenty years of St Joseph's where Sisters, who have served for decades in other houses in the Province and in Japan, Malaysia, Singapore, Australia and the Americas, can spend their days with their friends and provide a powerhouse of prayer for the wider IJ family, and for the peoples of the world, whether Christian, Hindu or Muslim.

> Even though this is a nursing home, there is openness and hospitality. Mairéad and Gertie are wonderful the way people can come in and out. I think we're different in that respect, more open, more inclined to integrate with people.[42]

While there is the same open house that is characteristic of the IJs, the Sisters have the security of knowing that they are under the watchful eye of Sr Mairéad O'Sullivan, Sr Gertie Lalor and, since her return from Tokyo, Sr Clare O'Callaghan.

---

[41] IJAD, Newsletter December 1989.
[42] Sr Peggy Murphy, interview with the authors, July 2008.

Willow Drive, Ballincollig 1985

Sr Elizabeth Browne returned to Ireland in 1982, after thirty years in Singapore, and was one of the pioneers who moved into Willow Drive in 1985 along with Sr Gemma O'Dwyer and Sr Nora Hartnett. The Annals show that they all immersed themselves in parish work: Sr Gemma visited the elderly, and took Holy Communion to the sick; Sr Nora worked with young people; Sr Elizabeth worked with adults, running prayer groups and parenting groups as well as offering tuition to primary school pupils from disadvantaged homes. Over the next twenty-five years Sr Elizabeth was the constant presence. She has been joined by other Sisters, including, Sr Mary Carmody (1989), Sr Louise Roche (1992), Sr Theophane (Annie Murphy, Crookstown, Co. Cork) (1997), Sr Fidelma Hogan (1997), Sr Sheila (O'Donoghue, Cork) (1999), Sr Evelyn (Houlihan, Kilmallock, Co. Limerick) (2000), Sr John Bosco O'Riordan (2000), Sr Margaret Mary Corbett (2000). Sr Rosario McAuliffe came here from Dromcollogher in 2000, and Sr Frances Dwane in 2008 after almost forty years in Widnes and Liverpool.

Glincool 1991

In preparation for the closing of Drishane, two bungalows, numbers 8 and 9 Glincool Gardens, were bought in Ballincollig, as part of a strategy to cluster smaller houses:

> After weeks of apprehension, packing, letting-go and burning, we – Sisters Andrew (Maud Spillane, Cork), Evangelist (Nellie Daly, Dromtariffe, Co. Cork), Isabelle (Margaret Gavin, Mount Bellew, Co. Galway), Vincent (Mary McSweeney, Crookstown, Co. Cork) and Zita (Nora Buckley, Mallow, Cork) – had still enough luggage for the trailer provided by Patrick and Michael Daly, who joined the cortege of cars bringing us to Glincool.[43]

But the next day, the Annals already record the question being posed by the Sisters:

> What is to be our involvement here for the rest of our journey to God? Then the thought, "Presence and prayer, deepening our union with Our Lord, listening to the Holy Spirit so that we can respond to the needs of those around us."

The Annals record constant interaction between the Sisters in the Ballincollig houses, as invitations are accepted and reciprocated. Also, the Sisters are invited back to Drishane on several occasions. They are made very welcome by their neighbours on the estate; they enjoy extending and receiving hospitality. In September 1992, the Annals announce A New Beginning, as Sr Máirín Campbell ('a Sister of many parts') and Sr Cecilia Cronin ('our driver') arrive to extend and renew the community.

In 2003, the community consisted of Sr Sheila O'Donoghue, Sr Dolores Healy, Sr Helen Hennessy, Sr Catherine Golden, Sr Zita Buckley and Sr Máirín Campbell. Sr Zita was the first to go and was later joined by Sr Catherine in Mallow. Sr Sheila and Sr Dolores moved to St Joseph's where Sr Máirín joined them. Sr Helen was assigned to the Millstreet community. These changes took place gradually and preparations began for the vacating of the house.

---

43 IJAD, *Glincool Annals*, 1991-2001.

Cherry Walk, Ballincollig 1993

Sr Carmel McMahon and Sr Killian (Helena O'Donoghue, Glandore, Co. Cork) were the pioneers in Cherry Walk in 1993. Sr Mary Carmody, who continued to live in Myross Wood until the IJ involvement there ended in 1994, was also part of the community. Officially 'the Cherries and the Willows' constituted one community with Sr Catherine Golden as Animator. Sr Agatha Ahern came here from Upton in 1995. She described the community's ministry for the Annals in 2003:

> A highlight of our ministry in Cherry Walk is the Galilee Prayer Group which meets on Tuesdays from 8 to 10 pm. The spiritual and social aspect of this meeting is very evident because the number of men and women who attend varies from 15 to 25 or more. A prayerful and caring concern for each member is tangible. All are aware of this.

They were also involved in visiting a nursing home in the parish, doing simple exercises to music, taking a special interest in each one, making sure there are 'no nobodies'. They visited people living alone, doing some chores for them and giving them reading materials. As well as going out to the parish community, Sr Agatha added: 'We are happy that our house is open to all who wish to come in!'

TRALEE

Cluain Íosagáin

On the 25th May 1987, when Sr Norrie and Sr Nellie (O'Sullivan) moved into rented accommodation at 2 Basin View, Tralee, they were already well in their seventies. However, their activities are listed as

> Running clubs for the elderly; craftwork at St John of God Centre with mildly handicapped; visitation of the housebound; Eucharistic ministry; folk dancing and PE with Primary children; housekeeping and correspondence with past pupils on the missions.[44]

When the owner looked for his house back, they were given a parish house at 44 Knockmoyle until it was needed for Canon Browne who was retiring from Millstreet. Finally, the Province purchased a house for them on St Brendan's Road, which they named Cluain Íosagáin. They were joined there by Sr Eithne McCarthy from North Circular Road who immediately became involved in the St Vincent de Paul Society. An entry for 24th September 1992 records that Sr Norrie went to the Mercy Convent for her first weekly folk-dancing lesson with Standard Five. Sr Mairéad O'Sullivan had spent several years in the Community when she was elected Provincial Superior and had to move to Clontarf in 1993. Shortly afterwards, Sr Mary Cotter joined the community.

20 Blackrock

On the 29th February 1992 a new Community was founded in Tralee. The pioneers were Sr Fintan McAuliffe, Sr Helen Keane, Sr Frances (Day, Whitegate, Co. Cork) and Sr Ita Higgins. Sr Fintan and Sr Helen Keane had both spent over thirty-five years in California; Sr Ita Higgins had spent over twenty years in Malaysia and Sr Frances Day had been in Drishane for some of its closing years. Sr Angela Buckley had also spent thirty years in Malaysia when she joined the Community. Sr Gertrude Finn came in 1997.

---

44 IJAD, Sr Norrie, typescript, Cluain Íosagáin.

Sr Frances is Chaplain in Tarbert Community School. She is a qualified psychotherapist who thoroughly enjoys her job and the scope it gives her to work with young people. She is also Chair of the Diocesan Pastoral Council, involved in strategic planning for the diocese, which now involves, among other things, clustering of parishes. She is very committed to the Kerry Adolescent Counselling Service, which makes counselling available to 12-18 year olds. It is funded by congregations and schools:

> In my community here in Tralee, two Sisters are over 80 and one is over 90. They would give you hope and confidence... Sr Gertrude is 96 on the 26th February. She goes to the Old Folks Home to feed the elderly, as she says herself. She walks over and back. She plays cards twice a week. I'd be gone to bed myself – I just check that she's in and the light is off![45]

7 Blackrock

The two Healy sisters, Sr Dolores (Mary) and Sr Josephine (Catherine), moved back to their native Tralee in 2001. Sr Dolores had been more than fifty years in Singapore and Sr Josephine forty years. After they moved out to St Joseph's in Cork, Sr Helen Wynne came in 2006. Sr Helen had held various posts during her career as an educator, including teacher, lecturer, and Headmistress of St Maur's in Weybridge. She is now involved in various artistic and literary pursuits in the diocese.

WEYBRIDGE CLOSING

MALLOW

> We, Sisters of the Infant Jesus, St Maur's Convent, Weybridge, took possession of our new home in Bellevue, Mallow, County Cork, on the 1st November 1997, after the keys of the bungalow had been officially handed over to Sr Mairéad, the acting Provincial, on 1st September.[46]

These are the opening words of the Annals of the community in Mallow and they sum up the reason for the founding of this house. The decision had been taken to move out of Weybridge and consultation had taken place with the Sisters on a possible new home for them. The house and setting are lovingly described:

> The workmen were still engaged in extending the building to provide ground-floor accommodation as well as a bright oratory overlooking the river Blackwater. A small lawn slopes down to the river and the paved pathways surrounding the house afford walking-space for the elderly. In the oratory, an oval-topped wooden altar and pedestal for the tabernacle, together with wall-rests for the Weybridge statues of Our Lady and St Joseph were fashioned by Dan Duggan, an old retainer and craftsman from Drishane.

---

[45] Sr Frances Day, interview with the authors, January 2009.
[46] IJAD, *Mallow Annals*.

The following are the Sisters listed as the pioneers in Bellevue:

Sr Ita McSweeney, who had first gone to Weybridge in 1932 and, apart from 1970-78 in the Isle of Wight, had spent all her life there; Sr Mary Lunt, who had gone to Malaysia in 1936, Thailand in 1958 and had spent the previous eighteen years in London; Sr Marie Noel (Mary Fitzgerald, Tralee, Co. Kerry), who had first gone to Weybridge in 1936 and, apart from nine years in Ireland, had been there ever since; Sr Bernard (Maureen Casey, Lurgan, Co. Armagh), who had first gone to Weybridge in 1945; Sr Canice (Margaret O'Connell, Kilnamartyra, Co. Cork), who had spent the previous twenty-six years in Weybridge; Sr Gobnait (Nora O'Connell, Kilnamartyra, Co. Cork), who had been in Weybridge, including Rosslyn House, for fifty years; Sr Louise Roche, who had spent fifteen years in America and twenty-five in Dublin and Cork. The 'devoted efforts' of Sr Mairéad O'Sullivan, Sr Beatrice Ahern, Sr Martha Hickey and Sr Louise Roche are credited with providing all with a beautiful, warm and comfortable first Christmas in their new home. The welcome from the priests, Sisters and parishioners, and the visits of congregational family as well as many old friends and past pupils of Drishane and Weybridge likewise contributed to the general atmosphere.

ENGLAND

WOKING 1969

In 1954, St Dunstan's School was opened in Woking. It began on a very small scale with just twenty-eight pupils and two Sisters: Sr Conrad (Nora Irwin, Cork City) and Sr Imelda (Joan O'Neill, Lattin, Co Tipperary) who travelled every day from their large Community base in St Maur's in Weybridge. In 1968, following the departure of the Providence Sisters from Woking, the decision was taken to open a house there. And so, on April 23rd 1969, the Pioneers arrived in Nine Oaks: Mother Philip (Catherine Golden), Sr Mark (Dianne Passalaqua, California), Sr Colman, Sr Marie-Bernard (Ita Noonan, Milford, Charleville, Co. Cork), Sr Martina (Bernadette Cadogan, Skibbereen, Co. Cork), Sr Laurence (Pauline Hannon, Ballitore, Co Kildare), Sr Ursula (Mainey, Dublin). The excitement of moving into a new place is conveyed in the Annals:

> Had some terrific days organising, remodelling, painting, furnishing etc. Since the house was idle for two years, hard work went into it during the first summer.

The Drishane Annals report the moving of the Novitiate here the following month:

> May 12th 1969: The last of the novices and young professed leave for Woking, Surrey with Sr Beatrice Ahern, novice mistress. There, they will do the juniorate, spiritual year; and any postulants who present themselves in the province will live in community in secular dress. The novitiate in Drishane is temporarily unoccupied, so we feel a sense of loneliness at losing the young sisters; from the beginning of Drishane, the novitiate has been an integral part of the convent here. We hope to see many young sisters returning here in due course. DV.

This is an important move, in the spirit of the Second Vatican Council. The system of Formation was one of the features of religious life which was changed utterly by the Council and the Novitiate as established in Drishane in 1909 – the principal motivation for founding Drishane itself – was never to be the site of Formation again.

In the new academic year, some Sisters continued to teach in St Dunstan's, while Sr Bríd (Mary de Courcy MacDonnell) and Sr Perpetua (Kathleen Day) started teaching in the new Catholic Secondary School. From the beginning, parish visitation was an important part of the Sisters' weekly activities. The Annals also noted that some Sisters reverted to their baptismal names at this time. On August 31st 1971, the Annals record 'a tearful day at Nine Oaks as we saw ten sisters off to Crewe.'

In September 1972 the Annals record 'the community completed': Sisters Daniel (Ita O'Connor, Mallow, Co Cork), Marie Edith (Baker, Surrey), Eileen (Margaret Lane, Caherdowney, Co Cork), Conrad, Cecile Butler, Zita, Georgina, Elizabeth (Duggan, Millstreet, Co. Cork), Edward (Nancy O'Donoghue, Cork), Anne (O'Neill, Ballineen, Co. Cork), Ita Noonan, Gemma (Marie Therese O'Sullivan, Valencia Island, Co Kerry), Pius (Eileen Singleton, Cullen, Co Cork), Mary (Hennessy, Cloyne, Co Cork), Maria (Mary Gallagher, Cork) and Frances Day. The work being undertaken is marked by its diversity. It was a very lively house, with people coming and going from various colleges and courses, visitors entertaining and being entertained, including Anglican Sisters, women's groups from the parish, as well as IJ Sisters from Weybridge, Crewe and Widnes.

In 1974 the following document is inserted in the Annals:

> This is to certify that on the 26th day of April, in the year of Our Lord nineteen hundred and seventy-four, Reverend Mother Philip Golden, on the anniversary of her religious profession, being in her twenty-fifth year of her membership of the Congregation of the Sisters of the Infant Jesus, otherwise known as the Dames of Saint Maur, formerly called the Congregation of the Charitable Mistresses, and being in the sixth year of her provincialate of the above-mentioned congregation, to commemorate the celebrations of praise and thanksgiving held in the Convent of Nine Oaks, Hook Heath Road, Woking, Surrey, in the presence of the Right Reverend Canon Aston, Dean of this diocese, of Reverend Mother Gabriel, former Provincial of the above-named congregation, of Reverend Mother Marie, revered and welcome visitor from Thailand, of Reverend Mother Daniel, Superior of the Community of Sisters at the said convent, and of all the community, planted, in the front lawn of Nine Oaks Convent, one magnolia tree, to be allowed to grow in perpetuity to her glorious memory and the pleasure of all members of the community and visitors thereto. It is to be cared for by the illustrious gardener, Sr Marie Edith, whose skill in such matters of horticulture is matched only by her virtue.
>
> We order that this certificate be carefully kept in the Archives of the above-mentioned convent. AD MULTOS ANNOS.

The document, while being playful, is nevertheless intended as a lasting testament to the high regard in which Mother Philip (Sr Catherine Golden) is held by her Community, all of whom signed it. However, she was not happy to discover some years later that the Woking Annals for 1975, 1976 and most of 1977 would appear not to have been kept.

Mission Sunday October 23rd 1977: It seems a pity not to record what goes on in our life, so that in times to come others can look back at religious life in the '70s. These are times of renewal and change when the future is being shaped; it is only in retrospect that we are aware often of the extent and rapidity of it all.

The account which follows in the Annals is a summary of the diverse activity being undertaken by the Woking community and represents a snapshot of religious community life in the post-Vatican II era.

Looking at the Province, the most obvious feature is the number of new foundations with small communities – even ones, twos and threes working in parishes, retreat houses and hostels. Our own community now consists of fourteen members but it exemplifies the same pluralism in its works. We are experiencing the way of life where some of our sisters come and go, working away from home, living in other Christian communities during the week.

Sr Edward continues to do night duty in the Methodist home for the elderly down the road – this contact with other Christians is one contribution to ecumenism. Woking is strong in its effort to work and pray for Christian unity. There is a Woking Central Churches Group, of which Fr Neville is chairman. Recently they had their annual day of prayer here at Nine Oaks, more than 30 people, ministers and lay and including two Anglican Sisters, attended. From time to time we attend the ecumenical services held in Woking in one of the many Christian churches.

Sr Pius and Sr Mary (Coleman, Kinsale, Co. Cork) work in London from Monday to Friday, returning for weekends. This is probably new in religious life and has to be considered in our efforts to build our religious community today. Sr Pius works in a hostel for overseas students. Her vast experience in Malaysia is of invaluable help in understanding and welcoming students from the East. Her work includes meeting newcomers, visiting them in their places of work, organising outings and socials for them, taking them on pilgrimage to Lourdes and generally being available to them. The weekly prayer meeting helps to form them in their Christian faith.

Sr Mary's work is to promote and coordinate youth clubs in the Westminster diocese. It involves a great deal of travelling, meeting priests, attending meetings, making reports. It is demanding and tiring work but answers a great need in our cities today.

Sr Philip's work for the diocese is also answering an urgent need today for Adult Religious Education. This involves travelling around the diocese, setting up centres for courses, arranging speakers and publicity, attending meetings often late at night. One of the saddest aspects of life in the 1970s in England is the breakdown in family life and the diocese is now beginning a programme of education and formation in an effort to support and prepare for family life.

Other members of the community carry on our traditional works of teaching, visiting, studying, running the house and welcoming people who call. At weekends there are religious instruction classes in Woking[47] and in Sutton Green. The community takes an active part in all parish functions such as new parishioners' meetings, parish council, first communion receptions, youth activities, garden fetes.

Our community timetable takes into account the fact that so many of us are out during the day. Private prayer is arranged by each individual. Morning prayer at 7.10

---

[47] RE classes given by Sr Zita Buckley and Sr Lucy (Brigid Burns, Cahirciveen, Co Kerry) who was awarded a Papal *Bene Merenti* for her long years of service to the Church.

is followed by Mass at 7.30. A quick breakfast followed by a hurried exodus leaves
the house relatively peaceful. Evening prayer follows our meal at 6.00. We now have
two sub-groups in community who meet to pray and share together at weekends. At
present we are pondering over the documents of our General Chapter. From time to
time we have a weekend or day retreat for ourselves. We are still fortunate enough
to have a confessor who comes to the house every few weeks and the use of the Revised
Rite of Penance has proved to be a great help to us all. We are richly supplied with books,
tapes and magazines and from time to time attend lectures to help our ongoing formation.

As I write the 5th Synod of Bishops is in progress in Rome on the subject of catechetics,
of particular interest to us whose aim is to make Jesus Christ known and loved. To
date the important ideas emerging are the need to take into account the situation and
culture of the people, the need to train and prepare catechists, the importance of small
groups and community, the responsibility of all Christians for the formation of the young,
the balance required between doctrinal formulation and living experience and above
all the centrality of the Mystery of Christ to all catechesis.

From then on the Annals are meticulously kept. Diversification continued in the apostolate.
For instance in October 1979 Sr Raphael (Brigid Bolger, Wexford) and Sr Bernadette (Doran,
Galway) joined the Community. Sr Raphael had spent fifty years in Malaysia and her
spirit of prayer was welcomed in the Community. Sr Bernadette, having spent thirty years
teaching in a big mixed school in France, on her retirement took up a new and interesting
apostolate in London Airport-Heathrow where she was affiliated to the Interdenominational
Chaplaincy. In the same month at least thirty Sisters went to the airport to see off Sr Ann
Marie Ryan and Sr Anne on their mission to Beagle Bay, Australia. They had Mass in the
airport chapel, the Annals record, 'their leaving was really a triumph.' Fr Bernard Barlow
OSM, National Secretary of the Mission Secretariat, who celebrated that Mass, wrote a
piece in the local paper on the personal cost of leaving home to spread the Good News in
distant lands:

> I reflected on how strange are the Lord's ways, how mysterious his designs. Here
> were two young women, very close to their own families, who had built up many
> friendships in the course of their apostolates in England and who had now responded
> generously to the call of the Lord to make even more sacrifices than the already heavy
> demands of modern religious life. They had been asked to preach the Gospel and
> minister to God's people in a bush area of Northern Australia which we would literally
> call today a "God-forsaken region." No longer would the area be without God. The Good
> News would be preached and the seeds of the Faith would be sown.[48]

On February 28th 1982 it was announced that the Sisters were to leave the parish. They
left in June:

> ...bringing with them the happiest of memories of the years spent here – a wonderful
> spirit of kindness exists in the community. However, it is God's plan that Nine Oaks
> should close and the Sisters will give of their best wherever God's will places them.

---

[48] IJAD, *Woking Annals.*

WIDNES 1970

The opening of the house in Widnes, on the 13th November 1970, is recorded with the same air of joy, excitement and readiness to take up a new challenge as Woking the previous year and this is repeated in all the other houses opened in the post-Vatican II era. Once again, Sisters from the other communities send welcoming messages:

> What joy to receive good wishes from every house in the Province, either by telegram or cards![49]

Some of them – in this case Sr Vincent McSweeney and Sr Margaret Elgin from Newsham Drive in Liverpool – welcomed the new arrivals in person. Sr Gemma O'Dwyer came from Woking to give a precious week of her time to help them settle in. The five pioneers in 1970 were Sr Mairéad O'Sullivan, Sr Ita Noonan, Sr Aquinas (Margaret Riordan, Millstreet, Co. Cork), Sr Majella (Eileen Holland, Enniskeane, Co. Cork) and Sr Theodora (Joan) Scannell. Sr Henry (Winifred Hogan, Rathcannon, Kilmallock, Co. Limerick) replaced Sr Theodora early in 1971.

But the story had begun fifteen years earlier, when Dean Hayes invited the IJ Sisters to Widnes. At first, they lived in a cottage in the grounds of St Bede's Parish Church. Mother General did not approve of this living arrangement – this being the 1950s before the Second Vatican Council and the era of small communities – and insisted that they live in their community in Liverpool. So they had to be taxied in and out every morning and evening. Over the years a steady procession of Sisters was involved in Fisher More Secondary Modern, listed as, Sisters Noreen Vaughan, Celestine, Senan, Mairéad, Margaret Mary Ryan, Bríd de Courcy MacDonnell, Mary Murphy, Perpetua (Kathleen Day), Luke (Margaret Walsh, Ballinascarty, Clonakilty, Co. Cork), Frances Day, Julie (Bromley, Wolverhampton); and Sr Joan Scannell listed as being in St Joseph's.

Sr Noreen Vaughan went to Liverpool when she qualified as a Domestic Science teacher and taught in Fisher More in Widnes. She found it a huge culture shock: the large numbers with the noise and confusion they caused, as well as the move to England. She has warm memories of Sr Mary Murphy who was there at the time: 'Sr Mary was very good to the children and really fantastic to us (the young Sisters). She was so kind, and helped us so much!'

Sr Noreen recalls travelling by taxi in silence from Liverpool in the 1960s:

> We were not allowed – by our own Congregation – to go into the staff room. So they converted a store room for us where we had our lunch – in silence! When it transpired that the staff could not tell one of the Sisters from another, the Headmistress put her foot down: "Go and tell your Superior that I want you in the staffroom with the rest of the staff!" Permission was eventually granted with the proviso that we couldn't sit in armchairs.[50]

The establishment in 1970 of the first small community in Widnes made for a big improvement in the Sisters' lives and also meant that they could be involved in the life of

[49] IJAD, *Widnes Annals.*
[50] Sr Noreen Vaughan, interview with the authors, January 2009.

the people. Sr David (Catherine Curtin, Freemount, Co. Cork) combined nursery teaching with parish work. Sr Ann Marie Ryan, and later Sr Julie, taught in Our Lady's Junior School. After working with the Aborigines in Australia, Sr Ann Marie returned in the late 1980s and joined the staff at St Basil's school. She also enriched St Basil's church liturgy through her gifts as a musician (as Julie did in Our Lady's), leading one of the music groups. Meanwhile, another Sister was getting involved with a different kind of music, as reported in the local newspaper:

> A young Widnes nun has become the 'manager' of an all-boy pop group. Now, the six-strong members of the teenage group, 'The Grasshoppers', are finding that Irish teacher-nun, Sr Mairéad, has a lot of sound advice to offer to help them become a professional act. Over the past twelve months Sr Mairéad has even got permission from her Superior for the boys to practise in their convent. 'When I heard that the lads were forming a pop group I asked them would they like to play at a family folk Mass at Our Lady's Church. They agreed and from then on I have tried to help them all I can. I suppose you could say I have become their 'manager' in a way. When they were looking for somewhere to practise I asked my Sister Superior could they come to the convent. She was pleased to help...The lads have improved very much.' Said 17-year-old rhythm guitarist, David Stagg: 'Sr Mairéad has been a great help to us. She has encouraged us to play and given us a lot of confidence. If we do get the chance to turn professional we will owe a lot to Sister.[51]

Reminders to the reader of the changes that have occurred in the Liturgy and the drive to become familiar with the documents of Vatican II occur frequently in the Annals:

> Mother Philip invited us in to Liverpool for a talk on the religious life which she gave to the two communities... We had the privilege of getting Holy Communion in the palms of our hands and of going on the altar to drink the wine from the Chalice.[52]

Another legacy of the Council, ecumenism, is evident in the Sisters' activities:

> On January 18th [1972] five Sisters went to the Wesley Methodist Church to join in prayer in union with people of other religious beliefs for the unity of all those who are baptised in Christ. There were about three hundred people present and one got a feeling and especially from the tone of the non-Catholic speakers that there was a real desire for unity. A Benedictine priest from Warrington preached the sermon. The prayer was led by Rev. J Douglas Johnson, Minister of Wesley Methodist Church. The Lesson was read by Rev. Shaw, Minister of Congregational Church and another lesson was read by Rev. Dean Donnelly, Catholic Dean of Widnes. Our religious beliefs were more or less mixed; still our hearts were united in one desire for union.

The Widnes community welcomed missionary Sisters when they returned from many years' service in Singapore, Malaysia, Japan and Australia. In 1973 Sr Finbar (Agnes Harrington, Eyeries, Co. Cork) joined the community. She had spent forty-six years in Malacca and now devoted her time to visiting the sick and the elderly in their homes in Our Lady's parish, bringing joy and consolation to so many people. However, on the 11th March 1976 she dropped dead. 'The members of the SVP formed a guard of honour and carried the coffin to the altar. The church was packed and everybody was shocked.' She is buried in Widnes, as is Sr Henry who worked as a parish sister in St Basil & All Saints from 1971 until 1984. Sr Henry was described by the parishioners as 'a walking saint' who carried on her ministry

---

[51] IJAD, Widnes box, *Catholic Pictorial*, 1st August 1971.
[52] IJAD, *Widnes Annals*, September 1971.

of visiting the sick, the poor and the bereaved, even while she herself was seriously ill with cancer. She was joined by Sr Margaret Mary Corbett who, after twenty-four years working as a missionary in Malaysia, came to Widnes in 1977. In 1985, Sr John Bosco came after thirty-six years in Malaysia. When they both returned to Ireland in 2000, the house in Widnes closed. The Annals end with the words of Père Barré: 'Whatever happens, be always at peace and trust in God.'

CREWE 1971

On Sunday 29th August 1971 the Annals record that the first three members of the Crewe community came to 47 Delamere Street to take up residence and begin the work of serving the people of God in this town. They were Sr David (Catherine Curtin, Freemount, Co Cork), Sr Melissa (KilBride, Kanturk, Co Cork) and Sr Claire (Murray, Cork). Sr Mairéad and other members of the Widnes community had the house in order for them, having worked hard at it all through the summer. The next day Sr Melissa and Sr Claire went to their schools and the following day the rest of the community arrived: Sr Beatrice Ahern, Sr Helen Coleman, Sr Georgina Clarson, Sr Frances Day, Sr Evelyn Foyle and Sr Aileen Murphy (Castlemagner, Co Cork). Fr Fallon outlined the work he would like them to do: visitation; religious instruction; teaching catechism in Sunday schools; teaching in schools; 'something for the Mums', youth clubs, etc. Unfazed by this list, the Sisters set about providing all of these services, and more, in his parish. Sr Hilary joined the Crewe community from the USA in 1988. As in other houses, the Annals record events in public life:

> Our prayers go out to Liverpool's bereaved folks after 95 fans were killed in a football match crush at the barrier in Sheffield. Everyone is deeply saddened. God rest the young and old who died. One boy of 14 carried a donor card and when he died in hospital his organs saved the lives of five people... we had a TV service from the Anglican Cathedral Liverpool to commemorate the dead and injured of Hillsborough disaster. The service was ecumenical and must have brought consolation to the shocked-looking congregation.[53]

Otherwise, the Annals report regular work with the elderly in the parish as well as with evangelization. There are frequent references to baptisms of adults as well as of babies. On the 7th May 1994, the Annals record:

> It is the end of a 23-year era for Crewe, alas! No date for closure as yet, but we are ready in our hearts... discernment, prayer and dialogue opened up the idea. We are sorry, but realise we could not continue. God has other plans.

It is this acceptance of God's Providence that characterises the response of the Sisters to all the major changes in their lives and their activities which the post-Vatican II era brought.

NEWBURY 1974

Sr Matthew (Margaret Lyons, Kilrush, Co Clare) had a brother living in Newbury. On her way back from Malaysia, where she had spent over fifty years, she stayed with her brother.

---

[53] IJAD, *Crewe Annals*, 21st-29th April 1989.

(She got her first guitar lessons from a tutor here and went on to teach guitar when she moved to Malahide.) The people loved her; she was so open and friendly and related easily to them. When the parish priest met Sr Matthew he expressed an interest in having Sisters in his parish. And so the story of the IJ involvement in Newbury began. Miss Smyth, who lived next door to the church, at 107 London Road, had retired to a home and had bequeathed her house to the parish. The parishioners had it repaired for parish use:

> The Sisters will live there rent free until you are able to appoint there one or two members of the Community who will be capable of earning wages in their professional work in the area.[54]

According to the agreement, it was the Sisters' responsibility to see to the upkeep of the house. Its central location helped the Sisters to integrate very quickly into the life of the parish. Sr Thomas (Mary Gilmore, Dunmore, Co Galway) and Sr Kate O'Neill came to Newbury in June 1974. Sr Kate worked as the district midwife which gave her access to many family homes. One parishioner remarked: 'I think she has done more for Christian Unity than many a sermon.'[55]

He was referring in particular to her presence at his baby's baptism in the Anglican Church. Sr Thomas had a pastoral ministry from the start caring for all classes of people, but especially the poor. 'She was an angel of mercy in Newbury, an absolute angel.[56']

In September they were joined by Sr Eilish O'Mahony and Sr Ann Marie Ryan. They had just made their final vows: Sr Ann Marie had a teaching post in the local Catholic primary school and Sr Eilish in a comprehensive school some distance from Newbury. So they were self-sufficient from the start and no burden on the parish. They ran courses on Knowing your Faith and kept open house at 107 London Road.

A newspaper article under the heading, The Busy Lives of Six Newbury Nuns, describes the six Sisters in the house at the time:

> Kate is just like any other midwife working locally for the Berkshire Health Authority. She is attached to Sandleford Hospital and during working hours she is to be found helping with deliveries or out on her rounds visiting mothers and newborn babies. Eilish works at Hurst School, Baughurst, where she teaches home economics... A third member of the community also does a fulltime job in addition to her religious work. She is Sr Ann Marie who teaches at St Joseph's school... Their ages span almost 50 years. The oldest is Sr Gabriel who at 71 proudly refers to herself as the 'grandmother' of the house. The others call her their VIP for she was once sister superior at a Weybridge convent and mother provincial for England and Ireland. Today she is enjoying a well-earned retirement. Sr Veronica (Valerie Freeman, Burnham, Essex) is a retired teacher who has worked, among other places, in Japan. She was there during the war and was taken prisoner by the Japanese. Her term of imprisonment lasted for three-and-a-half years. On her retirement she came to Newbury to help set up the community here. Her days are filled with visiting in the parish and she has just taken on the task of helping out with the administration of the volunteer centre. The sixth member of the community is Sr Thomas who was appointed sister-in-charge. It is her job to ensure the smooth running of the house. She sees that there is always someone there to welcome visitors and to give help and advice to those who call. The Sisters pride themselves on keeping 'open house' for all those who need them.

[54] IJAD, Derek Warlock, Bishop of Portsmouth, 28th September 1972.
[55] IJAD, parishioner quoted in Newbury file.
[56] Sr Catherine Golden, interview with the authors, July 2008.

Sadly, as various members of the community were called to other ministries, and those remaining were elderly, the decision had to be taken to close the house in 1992.

LIVERPOOL

The first house in Liverpool, Newsham Drive, was founded 'as a mission house' in the early 1950s. Mother Tarcisius instructed Sr Mary Lunt, who was home on leave at the time:

> 'Get permission to enter the diocese and buy a house.' When permission was granted, we found a three-storey house facing the park in Newsham Drive for £2,000. Sr Rosalie Griffin and I were sent to get it ready for the students and managed to buy the house next door for £2,500[57]

Sr Theophane Murphy came straight from Malaysia to be Superior there from 1953 to 1959. It was primarily a house for student Sisters, both from the mission countries and from England and Ireland. Some Sisters moved to Widnes when it opened in 1970 and, when Newsham Drive closed down in 1976, some Sisters went to a new house in Oakfield, Anfield. That house remained open for twenty years.

Meanwhile, in the post-Vatican II era, Fr Kevin O'Connor invited the Sisters to his parish, in the inner city area, St Anne's. The four pioneers in 1977 were Sr Catherine Fitzgerald, Sr Frances Dwane, Sr Rosalie (Nora Griffin, Killarney, Co. Kerry) and Sr Norrie O'Sullivan. They stayed in temporary accommodation in Edge Lane while awaiting a house from Merseyside Housing Association. Sr Maureen Roddy replaced Sr Rosalie in 1978; Sr Aileen Murphy replaced Sr Catherine Fitzgerald in 1981. The first meeting of Special Religious Development (SPRED) was held in 1982. SPRED is a network of services designed to assist persons with developmental or learning difficulties to integrate into parish life. Later two groups were formed, one for Juniors and one for Adults. In 1983 Sr Pauline Hannon joined the community and began teaching in the Junior School. Her mission in the school was closely linked to families and parish. At Christmas 1984, Sr Frances opened St Anne's Day Care Centre in a wing of the presbytery which she renovated and decorated herself. Its purpose was to befriend the housebound elderly and those with a handicap in the local community and to give them practical help. At Christmas 1985 the Christian Brothers and IJ Sisters prepared Christmas dinner at the Day Centre for the lonely people around who would otherwise have nothing. That was another successful new venture and became an annual event. In October 1986 Sr Antoinette joined the community as a student; in January 1987 Sr Ann Marie Ryan came for eighteen months and then Sr Raphael Moore. The house was closed in 1991.

Grinfield Street was bought with the Christian Brothers in 1991. The Christian Brothers lived on one floor, the IJ Sisters on another. The ground floor and the attic were used for all sorts of activities: there was a drop-in centre and also a big computer centre. Sr Frances Dwane had a wonderful understanding of people. Her approach was to ask them what they wanted and proceed to supply it, including chiropody. She believed in enabling rather than doling out. When she was leaving in February 2008, the Parish Priest expressed the appreciation and thanks of all the parishioners, particularly the elderly. Sr Frances, for her

[57] IJAD, Liverpool box. Sr Mary Lunt (handwritten note).

part, stressed the qualities of the people in the parish and how she was edified by them.[58] Sr Jo Cremin retired from her teaching post in 2008. A very committed teacher, who also taught in Malahide and Ballymun, she continues to be involved in education, helping children who need extra support.

EAST ACTON 1977

In 1977 the Province bought 16 East Acton Lane in London for £28,000. Later that year the community moved in from their temporary accommodation in a bungalow on Ealing Common. The pioneers were Sr Margaret Mary (Ryan, Garryshane, Donogh Hill, Co. Tipperary), Sr Louis Marie (Murphy, Togher Road, Cork), Sr Rosalie Griffin, Sr Imelda (Bridget Collins, Carrowmore, Ballina, Co. Mayo) and Sr Mary Hennessey. For various reasons, the original community had to be replaced the following year. Sr Mary Lunt went there in 1979 and stayed until she left for Weybridge in 1996, during which time she was Chaplain in Wormwood Scrubs Prison where she had remarkable rapport with the prisoners. She was joined by Sr Mary Coleman and Sr Mary Carmody. Sr Angela Buckley spent twelve years here. She ran the house and cooked for everyone, in between going out to visit the sick and elderly in the parish. Sr Fidelma Hogan was here from 1984, working in the Christian Meditation Centre in London, until 1995 when she was one of the pioneers in Dromcollogher. Sr Kitty (Ellard, Hornchurch, Essex) joined the community in 1986. Having been chaplain in the Polytechnic in Wolverhampton, Sr Kitty was appointed Co-ordinator of Third Level Chaplains. Then, when the Sisters left St Maur's in Weybridge, she was invited to take up the post of Chaplain in St George's College to maintain the IJ continuity. Sr Pat (Armato, San Francisco) had a serious decision to take in 1989 when the houses in her native California were closed. She opted for the English mission, moved to East Acton, and has been teaching in London for twenty years now. Sr Breda Madigan, having had her work in Nigeria cut short by a twelve-year period of service on the General Council, joined this Community in 2002. She is very involved in work for justice and peace. She keeps the Province informed, and encourages her Sisters to become active, on issues in this vital area of Christian activity.

WOLVERHAMPTON 1978

> I have felt for a long time that the call for renewal put out by Vatican II has been answered best by Religious, and would very much like to see it flow over into parish life. I am convinced that there is very important work to be done which is best tackled by women... You may well say all of this can be done by lay people or even the priest if he is not too lazy, but, to my mind, there is a value that can only be given by Religious which makes all the difference.[59]

The Sisters were not looking for a mission when Fr Molloy sent his appeal, but the Province gave an immediate response and two Sisters answered the call:

> I am interested in the Wolverhampton project, pending approval from Sr Theophane (my present Provincial, Japan); and, of course, approval from Sr Raphael [Provincial,

58 IJAD, Liverpool box.
59 IJAD, Fr Hugh Molloy, SS Peter & Paul Wolverhampton, 9th June 1977.

England-Ireland], who may have other plans for me according to the Lord's will.
In the Lord Jesus, Sr Odile (Kathleen O'Sullivan, Doneraile, Co. Cork).[60]

Sr Odile had just returned after almost thirty years in Yokohama. The other volunteer was Sr Marie Conheady coming from Liverpool. They took up residence on the 6th October 1977 in a flat off the Presbytery which proved providential, because in the months there they built up a team relationship with Fr Molloy and a good relationship with the other occupants of the Presbytery. The following February they moved into 38 Park Road East. Sr Odile was to be a much-cherished Chaplain of the Afro-Caribbean community of Wolverhampton for almost twenty years. Sr Eileen and Sr Mary Murray (formerly Sr Virgilius, Broadford, Co. Clare) – who was trying to decide whether or not to stay home from Japan – joined them there. Sr Frances Day had just graduated from Strawberry Hill and got a teaching job in Wolverhampton:

> That was a baptism of fire – a comprehensive with 1200 pupils. I loved it, and I loved the ministry to youth. I spent seven wonderful years there.[61]

Sr Kitty Ellard arrived the year after Sr Frances and stayed until 1986 when she moved to East Acton. The Sisters were feeling their way into this new ministry of 'being' in the parish.

> We see our house as the hub of our mission and we have planned it so that no matter what Sisters join the community they can be very actively involved in the apostolate on the spot.[62]

They realised that they were not social workers, nor should they try to be, but that their role was mainly a pastoral ministry and that the essential qualification was to be a sympathetic listener. They found that most people wanted to be listened to rather than advised. They were also very aware that they were fortunate in having a parish priest who was very concerned for their welfare, spiritual and material, and that they had the support of their own Sisters in the Province to sustain them. They were greatly appreciated by the people through their different ministries. These ministries included Hospital Chaplaincy, carried out by Sr Ann Breen and subsequently by Sr Mary (O'Connell, Tralee, Co. Kerry). Sr Mary's main ministry was to the Travellers, becoming their friend and their voice over a period of twenty years. Sr Paula (Alice) KilBride's ministry was Prison Chaplaincy in Featherstone. Meanwhile, the Sisters had moved to Merridale Road in 1984. From 1985, the Novitiate was based here with Sr Marie (Pitcher, Malahide, Co. Dublin) in charge of Formation. The idea was to provide novices with the opportunity to be involved in a variety of ministries alongside their training for religious life. Sr Mary Murray, herself a native of Wolverhampton, was part of that Novitiate and, in 2004, started working with excluded children:

> Excluded, that's the official term used, isn't it awful? They have emotional, social and behavioural problems and live very hard lives. Most, but not all, are in foster care, or their parents are on drugs, or there's violence... I make them laugh but I do get cross. Never to show I'm cross is not good. They have to know they've crossed the boundary because there are no boundaries at home. They live with all kinds of abuse and confusion. When you've calmed them you can work with them. We've had three go back into mainstream – that's the aim... They are Père Barré's children.[63]

---

[60] IJAD, Sr Odile [undated].
[61] Sr Frances Day, interview with the authors, January 2009.
[62] IJAD, *Wolverhampton Annals*.
[63] Sr Mary Murray, interview with the authors, January 2009.

Sr Marie Pitcher was elected Provincial Superior in 1999 and, following her six years in that position, was elected Institute Leader ('Mother General'). It is, indeed, Providential that, in the centenary year of Drishane, and fifty years after the founding of Malahide, a past pupil of Malahide should be serving as the second Irish Institute Leader of the Infant Jesus Sisters.

The Hope Community, Heath Town, 1986

Sr Margaret Walsh was teaching for nine years in a Catholic Comprehensive School in Crewe when a call to be more radically involved with the poor in the inner city led her to Wolverhampton in 1984.[64] She was asked, along with Sr Mary Joy (Langdon, Battle, Sussex) and Sr Mary de Courcy MacDonnell, by the local parish priest to undertake a census of Heath Town estate. When they knocked on people's doors for that purpose, they quickly were drawn into their stories; the census became secondary and they decided to join these people by becoming council tenants on the estate. During their first year, they were joined by men and women who wished to share their faith, their community life and their ministry in the area. And so The Hope Community was born. The Hope Family Project is a partnership project between the Infant Jesus Sisters and Father Hudson's Society.

From the outset they tried to be a loving and caring community themselves and also to work with others to build up community on the estate. The people living on the estate could hardly be described as a community, since they were marginalised and socially isolated, with over 80% on Social Benefit and nearly the same percentage in rent arrears. The environment was bleak with many tenants suffering from psychiatric disorders not knowing how to cope themselves and in no position to help their neighbours. They were confused by all the red tape and paper work required in order to claim their rightful benefits and would often go hungry for days before the cheque arrived.

> Attempting to do things for people tends not to be life-giving in the long run and perhaps is often a reflection of our own misguided need to be needed and our inborn tendency to dominate and so treat people as the objects of our charity. Only by walking alongside others and being with them can we grow into the type of community that Christ envisioned for his kingdom.[65]

They set no targets, drew up no agenda, but listened to the people and, like the Samaritan, 'abandoned their own road and moved into the path of the suffering traveller'. Rather than impose their own solutions on the situation, they aimed to encourage local leadership and to develop the Gifts of the Spirit, which the people have, and to find ways by which they can use these gifts in their own homes and in their community. This is far more time-consuming and requires far more patience than doing it for them. As far as converting the people of Heath Town is concerned, they believe that they can best meet their needs by helping them to recognise God in their own experience before they can meet Him in the sacramental life of the Church.

They also see the need to alert people to the deprivation, the poverty, the helplessness experienced in their midst which they very often are totally unaware of. This is an important

---

[64] IJAD, Sr Margaret Walsh, *Here's Hoping*, 1991.
[65] Ibid., 9.

part of their apostolate and is the key to changing the situation through a wider social and political awareness.

The Hope Family Centre has grown exponentially over the almost quarter of a century of its existence. The original ethos remains the guiding force for all undertakings. Seeking out the most vulnerable and isolated families remains at the top of its agenda, and supporting them in whatever way is appropriate. It is run by committed staff and volunteers and is funded from public and private sources, including the IJ Institute. The range of activities reflects the Centre's responsiveness to needs as they arise and as funding can be found. There are parent groups; groups for boys; groups for girls; social groups for adults; lunch club for the over 50s; support for asylum seekers and refugees and family support provided in the home. A new venture in 2008 is ESOL to provide English language classes for those who can't access them either through lack of provision or lack of confidence:

> Without these language skills people will remain isolated, hidden and often full of fear and anxiety about a strange and foreign world outside their own doors. Their children will be immediately disadvantaged when they begin school and are less likely to realise their full potential.[66]

And so another strand is added to the services being offered, bringing with it the need to train volunteers and prepare them for the particular difficulties associated with language learning. Already the Hope Family Community is planning ahead towards an intergenerational learning programme at a later stage.

Brushstrokes, Smethwick, 1998

> *We must be in the hand of God like a brush in the hand of the painter.*
>
> Nicolas Barré

In 1998, with the experience gained in Heath Town, the IJ Sisters, Fr Hudson's Society and St Philip's Parish met to discuss the possibility of setting up a similar project in Smethwick. Once again the focus was to be on solidarity with the most vulnerable and deprived people in the neighbourhood irrespective of faith, culture or background. The aim was to get to know them, earn their trust and uncover gifts and potential especially among those who felt worthless and without hope. In the beginning the work was mainly with families associated with the parish, the school and the local Sikh community, then refugees from Bosnia, then asylum seekers. After five years and much fundraising, a centre was opened in 2003:

> It was burnt down in an arson attack two months later. We didn't lose hope, and took inspiration from a quote from Nicolas Barré: *It is often in the valley of misfortune that God blesses us. One can see the stars shining more brightly from the bottom of a well than in full daylight from the ground above.* In August 2004, a much improved parish centre was reopened.[67]

The programme of activities in Smethwick is carried out by committed staff and volunteers and funded from public and private sources.

---

[66] IJAD, HFC Annual Report 2008.
[67] IJAD, Sr Margaret Walsh, *Brushstrokes Ten Years On*, 2008.

EASTBOURNE 1981

Sr Kate O'Neill accompanied by her mother, Kathleen O'Neill, arrived in August 1981 to take up residence in Maryland, Hampden Park, Eastbourne, where they were joined by Sr Bernardine Singleton. Sr Kate immediately took up the post of Macmillan Sister, caring for the terminally ill in their homes in association with St Wilfred's Hospice. Sr Bernardine began work as a Parish Sister and Catechist. She spent the last months of that year making contact with the parents of children attending non-Catholic schools who were at an age to prepare for First Holy Communion. She also visited the housebound in their homes. Sr Michael (Alice O'Regan, Kildorrery, Co Cork) joined them and moved in as the third member of the community the following February. Later that year, when Woking closed, they were delighted to welcome Sr Marie Edith as the fourth member of the community. Although their stay in Eastbourne was just over a decade, the Sisters made a real contribution to the people both through their work and through their presence among them.

Happily, in 2001, Sr Ita Noonan moved to Eastbourne to work as a Parish Sister, so there is once again an IJ presence there.

CRAWLEY 1981

In 1981, Sr Cecilia (Mary O'Shea, Glanmire, Cork) and Sr Mairéad O'Sullivan moved into 12 Eastwood. Until 1980 the Friary Parish in Crawley town centre was run by the Friars. When it was once again served by diocesan priests, the new parish priest, Fr Seamus Hester, invited the IJ Sisters to come and form a team with him. (He had worked with IJ Sisters in Woking previously.) It was a new, original idea then, the beginning of collaborative ministry. The Sisters moved into their current home, attached to the multipurpose building which is St Bernadette's church and hall. The pioneers brought creativity and enthusiasm to the project and were joined over the years by different Sisters and priests in the parish. Sr Agnes O'Connor joined the team in 1989 and Sr Ita Noonan in 1990, both having been in Australia. Sr Georgina Clarson came in 1996 from her mission in Cameroon and Nigeria. Margaret Holland, who was doing her Novitiate in Wolverhampton, came for three months' pastoral experience, and brought great youth and energy to the team. In early 1997, when Sr Mairéad visited as Provincial, she was also welcomed back as one of the pioneers. The Sisters were greatly encouraged by her response to their apostolate:

> Ita going regularly to the Gatwick detention centre ... Georgina going into Crawley College and involved in visiting Asian and African people in the parish. It is our way of bringing the IJ charism, helping the parish to reach out to those who may be marginalised.[69]

Then, when Weybridge was closing, St Bernadette's welcomed Sr Rosemary (Barter, Cork City), who was working in the Catholic Children's Society in Purley. Her initial contract with CCS was to investigate ways in which to respond to the emotional needs of children and young people through the school system. This led to her setting up and managing a Counselling Service for Primary and Secondary Schools and Sixth Form Colleges. She was

---

[68] IJAD, *Eastbourne Annals.*
[69] IJAD, *Crawley Annals.*

subsequently asked by the Board of Directors to take on the Chaplaincy at the Society. This enabled her to make contact with all the services offered – Adoption, Fostering, Residential work and Community-based centres.

> In all our work there is the constant thrust to continue to find ways of supporting those who live on the margins of society – the abandoned, the homeless teenagers, the abused, the bereaved, the refugees.[70]

In 2006, Sr Rosemary was elected Provincial Superior of England-Ireland.

SUNNINGDALE AVENUE 1989

Sr Fidelma and Sr Fabian took up residence in 30 & 32 Sunningdale Avenue in September 1989, even though the houses were only partly furnished. The painting continued for some months and the chapel was completed for Christmas. Sr Fidelma continued working in the Christian Meditation Centre while Sr Fabian was occupied as a member of the St Vincent de Paul Society. Sr Catherine Golden joined the Community in January 1990 and very soon became a member of the chaplaincy team of Pentonville Prison. Sr Mary Murray (Wolverhampton) came in September 1990 to do a course in Nursery Nursing for two years followed by an Adult Education Course for one year.

Sr Mary Joy Langdon came in 1992 and Sr Kate O'Neill in 1994. Sr Kate O'Neill started to work as a Marie Curie nurse. Having been nursing since 1957, first as a general nurse, then as a midwife, health visitor, geriatric nurse and a Macmillan nurse, she found this kind of nursing the most rewarding of her career. She also became a volunteer with the Samaritans where she was interviewed by a journalist:

> During the night shift, the phones were being staffed by a businessman and a nun – both charming, both very busy during the day. I asked the nun what she did for fun. "Oh, I work as a Marie Curie nurse tending the terminally ill." She was one of the most delightful women I've ever met – exactly the sort of person to whom you would want to open your heart.[71]

They are both active in the Parish: Sr Mary Joy is involved with liturgy preparation, including choir; Sr Kate is always on call to the needs of parishioners.

Wormwood Scrubs Pony Centre 1988

Of all the projects the IJ Sisters are involved in – and they are many and various – probably the most remarkable to the outside observer is the Pony Centre. Sr Mary Joy grew up with horses and, when she left school, developed her own equestrian business. After she joined the IJ congregation she was working at the London Light House, a centre for people with AIDS or HIV. After five years of being away from horses, she was encouraged by Sr Alice KilBride, who was Provincial Superior at the time, to use her equestrian skills and experience for the benefit of children and young people with special needs.

---

[70] IJAD, Crawley box, Sr Rosemary typescript, July 2004.
[71] IJAD, Imogen Stubbs, *Weekend Telegraph*, 13th February 1999.

It is truly a miracle how what was a very muddy patch of ground with no facilities such as electricity, toilets, telephone etc. has developed into today's centre. God indeed works in mysterious ways and amazing things can and do happen. I found myself without money, planning permission, without local licence, without council consent but I did have three Shetland ponies and enthusiasm.[72]

The Centre has now grown into a place where children from all backgrounds and with all abilities and disabilities are welcome. There are eighteen ponies and full indoor school facilities. The Centre offers therapeutic riding sessions and teaches children to care for animals. It also encourages children and young people to become volunteers and to help others. Young people are given the opportunity to gain qualifications; the Centre allows them to be involved in an outdoor physical activity in a healthy environment. Many city children, who have little experience of a rural environment, come to the Centre and learn about nature while experiencing rural life. Sr Mary Joy sees as one of the main missions of the Centre '...to help children to hold onto their innocence by allowing them to be with ponies in a safe and supportive environment.' She is passionate in her belief that children should enjoy their childhood to the full, whatever their abilities or disabilities.

[72] IJAD, Sr Mary Joy Langdon, Wormwood Scrubs Pony Centre typescript 2008.

ENGLAND - IRELAND PROVINCE 2009

DUBLIN
St Lawrence Road
Rosemary Barter

Clontarf Road
Ann Breen
Kathleen Day
Carmel O'Sullivan
Catherine O'Sullivan
Catherine Shanahan
Eileen Sheehan

Tonlegee Road
Margaret Cotter
Pauline O'Dwyer
Hilary O'Rourke

Ballymun
Malen del Valle Garcia
Catherine Lynch

Ballymun (Poppintree)
Ann Marie Ryan

Portmarnock
Eleanor Nevill
Noreen Vaughan

Eccles Court
Betty Kelleher

DROMCOLLOGHER
Joan Scannell

TRALEE
Blackrock No.20
Frances Day
Gertrude Finn
Ita Higgins
Helen Keane

Blackrock No.7
Helen Wynne

Cluain Iosagáin
Angela Barrett (Limerick)
Mary Cotter

CORK
St Joseph's
Enda Beasley
Máirín Cambell
Brendan Cronin
Dolores Healy
Josephine Healy
Helen Hennessy
Evelyn Houlihan
Gertie Lalor
Peggy Murphy
Clare O'Callaghan
Máiréad O'Sullivan

Willow Drive
Elizabeth Browne
Frances Dwane
Rosario McAuliffe

Cherry Walk
Agatha Ahern
Mary Carmody
Carmel McMahon

Mallow
Beatrice Ahern
Ann Crowley
Catherine Golden
Fidelma Hogan
Martha Hickey
Agnes Kiely
Paul O'Flynn
Louise Roche
Réidín Scannell

Millstreet
David Curtin
Peter Fahy
Helen Falvey
Attracta Gilmore
Emilie Nagle
Mary O'Connell
Florence O'Sullivan
Ailbe Sweeney
Margaret Tarrant

IRISH SISTERS IN OTHER PROVINCES

ENGLAND
Crawley
Hannah Murray

Crawley (Hexham Close)
Eilish O'Mahony
Marie Pitcher - Superior General

Eastbourne
Pauline Hannon (Southwick)
Ita Noonan

Horsham
Alice KilBride

East Acton Lane
Pat Armato
Kitty Ellard
Breda Madigan

Sunningdale Avenue
Mary Joy Langdon
Kate O'Neill

Smethwick
Margaret Walsh

Burton-on-Trent
Mary de Courcy MacDonnell

Liverpool
Jo Cremin

Weybridge
Mary Murphy

Wolverhampton
Mary Murray

CAMEROON
Noreen McGrath

CZECH REPUBLIC
Georgina Clarson
Veronica Řeháková

NIGERIA
Anne O'Neill
Antoinette O'Callaghan
Bernadette O'Reilly

SINGAPORE
Rosario Egan
Deirdre O'Loan

JAPAN
Paschal Baylon O'Sullivan
Carmel O'Keeffe

MALAYSIA
Aidan Fitzgerald

Simple in virtue, ste
Simple dans ma ve

Sr Agnes O'Connor

Sr Andrew Spillane

Sr Joan Scannell

Sr Ann Breen (Columban)

Sr Augustine O'Donovan

Sr Basil Halpin

*Sr Carmel O'Sullivan
(Maria Assumpta)*

Sr Catherine Lynch

...fast in duty

...forte dans mon devoir

Sr Eilish Ahern (Benignus)

Sr Consilia Quinn

Sr Florence O'Sullivan

Sr Edmund Sheehy

Sr Eilish O'Mahony

Sr Eithne McCarthy

Sr Etienne Hyland

Simple in virtue, ste

Simple dans ma ver

Sr Flannan Galvin

Sr Gertie Lalor (Pius)

Sr Helen Wynne

Sr Ita O'Connor (Daniel)

Sr James Walsh

Sr Kathleen Day

Sr Joseph Harty

fast in duty

forte dans mon devoir

Sr Kevin Dowling

Sr Máire Bríd Ward

Sr Mary Carmody

Sr Eleanor Nevill
(Richard)

Sr Mary Magdalen
McGillycuddy

Sr Mary Josephine Durkan

Sr Mary O'Sullivan

Sr Mary Murphy-
O'Connor

Simple in virtue, ste

Simple dans ma ve

Sr Mary Peter Weedle

Sr Monica Kelly

Sr Patricia Clarke

Sr Noreen Vaughan
(Dolores)

Sr Georgina Clarson

Sr Pauline Hannon
(Lawrence)

Sr Brendan Scollard

Sr Pauline Lenehan

fast in duty

forte dans mon devoir

Sr Betty Kelleher
(Christine)

Sr Agnes Kiely

Sr Eucharia O'Callaghan

Sr Teresa O'Donoghue

Sr Thomas Aquinas Forde

Sr Peter Fahy

Sr Reidín Scannell

Sr Cecile Butler

Simple in virtue, Ste
Simple dans ma ve

Sr Louise Roche

Sr Margaret Tarrant

Sr Leonie Redmond

M. St Etienne Flahault

Sr Killian O'Donoghue

M. St Anthony Coleman

Sr Perpetua O'Brien

Sr Jo Cremin (Colman)

fast in duty

forte dans mon devoir

Sr Raphael Moore
1974 - 77, 1983 - 86

Sr St Stanislaus
Wickham 1958

Sr Rosemary Barter
2005 -

Sr Alice KilBride
1987 - 93

Sr St Gabriel Browne
1959 - 68

Sr Carmel McMahon
1977 - 83

Sr Catherine Golden
1968 - 74

Sr Mairéad O'Sullivan
1993 - 99

Sr Marie Pitcher
1999 - 2005

LIST OF ILLUSTRATIONS

Abbreviations: IJAD: Infant Jesus Archive Dublin
IJAP: Infant Jesus Archive Paris

Page